YOUR recipe could appear in our next cookbook!

Share your tried & true family favorites with us instantly at

www.gooseberrypatch.com

If you'd rather jot 'em down by hand, just mail this form to...

Gooseberry Patch • Cookbooks – Call for Recipes
PO Box 812 • Columbus, OH 43216-0812

If your recipe is selected for a book, you'll receive a FREE copy!

Please share only your original recipes or those that you have made your own over the years.

Recipe Name:

Number of Servings:

Any fond memories about this recipe? Special touches you like to add
or handy shortcuts?

Ingredients (include specific measurements):

Instructions (continue on back if needed):

Special Code: **cookbookspage**

Over ➤

Extra space for recipe if needed:

Tell us about yourself...

Your complete contact information is needed so that we can send you your FREE cookbook, if your recipe is published. Phone numbers and email addresses are kept private and will only be used if we have questions about your recipe.

Name:
Address:
City: State: Zip:
Email:
Daytime Phone:

Thank you! Vickie & Jo Ann

Tasty Fall Cooking

Delicious and easy...recipes for every autumn
occasion from tailgating to Thanksgiving!

Gooseberry Patch

An imprint of Globe Pequot
246 Goose Lane
Guilford, CT 06437

www.gooseberrypatch.com

1•800•854•6673

Copyright 2016, Gooseberry Patch 978-1-62093-237-7

Do you have a tried & true recipe...

tip, craft or memory that you'd like to see featured in
a **Gooseberry Patch** cookbook? Visit our website at
www.gooseberrypatch.com and follow the
easy steps to submit your favorite family recipe.
Or send them to us at:

Gooseberry Patch
PO Box 812
Columbus, OH 43216-0812

Don't forget to include the number of servings your recipe makes,
plus your name, address, phone number and email address. If we
select your recipe, your name will appear right along with it...
and you'll receive a **FREE** copy of the book!

Contents

Dedication

To everyone who loves caramel apples, spiced pumpkin pies, roast turkey with dressing and all the other wonderful flavors of fall.

Appreciation

A heartfelt thanks to all who shared their best, most delicious harvest recipes.

Cozy
Breakfasts
to Share

Belgian Waffles

LaDeana Cooper
Batavia, OH

No need to purchase those boxed waffle mixes...here's a quick recipe and I'll bet you already have the ingredients! Dress up the waffles with fresh fruit and whipped cream. Or make chocolate waffles and add pecans and a drizzle of caramel sauce for a turtle waffle. Yum!

2-1/4 c. all-purpose flour
1/2 c. sugar
1 T. baking powder
3/4 t. salt
Optional: 1 T. baking cocoa

3 eggs, beaten
1-1/2 c. milk
1 c. butter, melted and slightly
   cooled
1 T. vanilla extract

In a bowl, mix together flour, sugar, baking powder and salt; add cocoa if making chocolate waffles. In a separate large bowl, whisk together remaining ingredients. Slowly add flour mixture to egg mixture; stir just until combined to form a thick batter. Ladle batter by 1/2 cupfuls, or as directed, into a preheated and greased waffle maker. Bake according to manufacturer's directions. Makes 6 or more waffles.

At fall farmers' markets and county fairs, watch for bottles of Grade B maple syrup. It isn't second-best...it's just a little darker color than Grade A! Also called cooking syrup, Grade B's deep maple flavor is ideal for using in recipes.

Cinnamon French Toast Dippers

Diana Chaney
Olathe, KS

*Little hands love to pick up these crisp golden French toast sticks!
Spoon a dollop of the sauce into a cup and top with toast sticks
for an easy-to-handle breakfast.*

4 eggs, beaten
1/2 c. vanilla Greek yogurt
1/4 t. cinnamon

4 thick slices day-old bread,
  each cut into 3 to 4 sticks
1 to 2 T. butter, divided

In a shallow bowl, whisk together eggs, yogurt and cinnamon until blended. Soak bread sticks in egg mixture, turning once. Melt one tablespoon butter in a skillet over medium heat. Working in batches as needed, add bread sticks to skillet. Cook until golden on both sides. Add remaining butter as needed. Serve French toast sticks with Maple Dipping Sauce. Serves 2 to 4.

Maple Dipping Sauce:

3/4 c. vanilla Greek yogurt
1/4 c. maple pancake syrup

1/8 t. cinnamon

Combine all ingredients; stir well.

Keep a tin of pumpkin pie spice on hand to jazz up pancakes,
muffins and coffee cakes. A quick shake adds cinnamon,
nutmeg and allspice all at once.

Tasty Fall Cooking

Baked Oatmeal Deluxe

Charity Schneider
Cheyenne, WY

Our family has made this recipe for years, and it's still a favorite, topped with canned peaches and milk. It works well as a quick breakfast before church on Sunday mornings. We especially enjoy it with blueberries, coconut and walnuts.

4 eggs, beaten
2 c. milk
1/2 c. oil
1 t. vanilla extract
1 c. brown sugar, packed
6 c. long-cooking oats,
   uncooked
4 t. baking powder

1 to 2 t. cinnamon
Optional: 1 t. nutmeg
1 t. salt
Optional: 1 to 2 c. canned sliced
   peaches, 2 c. blueberries,
   1 to 2 c. flaked coconut,
   1 c. chopped walnuts

In a large bowl, combine eggs, milk, oil, vanilla and brown sugar; mix well. Add oats, baking powder, spices, salt and desired add-ins; mix well. Pour into a greased 13"x9" baking pan. Bake, uncovered, at 350 degrees for 30 to 40 minutes. Makes 10 servings.

One year our family decided to rent a cabin in the Great Smoky Mountains for Thanksgiving. Early Thanksgiving morning, my parents, brothers, nieces, nephews and I tumbled out of bed and gathered to watch the parade. We had planned an extra special pancake menu for breakfast. Each of us women made a different kind of pancakes. We had buttermilk pancakes, pumpkin pie pancakes, blueberry pancakes and chocolate chip pancakes just to name a few. But the biggest hit by far were the yummy Elvis pancakes my niece Natalie made. She was in middle school, and had searched the internet to select her recipe. She measured the ingredients and made them with love. The pancakes were all delicious, but Natalie's pancakes were the sweetest!

–Monica Britt, Fairdale, WV

Apple Fritter Bites

Cassie Hooker
La Porte, TX

Whip up this delectable, quick & easy recipe for breakfast,
or serve with spiced cider for a party treat.

1-3/4 c. all-purpose flour	1 egg, beaten
2 t. baking powder	oil for deep frying
1 c. cooking apple, peeled, cored	Garnish: maple syrup,
and chopped	powdered sugar
1 c. milk	

In a large bowl, mix together flour and baking powder; add apple and set aside. In a separate bowl, stir together milk and egg. Add to flour mixture and stir just until moistened. Heat one to 2 inches oil in a deep fryer or heavy deep saucepan over medium heat. Working in batches, carefully drop batter into oil by tablespoonfuls. Cook 3 for 4 minutes, until golden, turning once while frying. Drain on paper towels. Serve fritters warm with syrup, sprinkled with powdered sugar, if desired. Makes 4 to 6 servings.

Nothing is quite as intoxicating as the smell of bacon frying in the morning, save perhaps the smell of coffee brewing.

–James Beard

Savory Sausage Muffins

Beckie Apple
Grannis, AR

These days, a home-cooked breakfast is almost a thing of the past. After experimenting, I came up with this recipe that I can make on weekends. Then, through the miracle of of the microwave, we can have a hot breakfast muffin all week long. A cup of hot coffee, a tub of soft-spread butter and a bottle of honey make this a savory breakfast.

1 lb. ground pork sausage
2 T. green pepper, chopped
1/2 onion, chopped
8-1/2 oz. pkg. corn muffin mix
7-3/4 oz. pkg. cheese & garlic
  biscuit baking mix

1/2 t. baking powder
2 eggs, beaten
3/4 c. milk
2 T. oil
1 c. shredded Cheddar cheese

In a skillet over medium heat, combine crumbled sausage, green pepper and onion; cook until sausage is no longer pink. Drain and set aside. Combine dry mixes, baking powder, eggs, milk and oil in a large bowl; mix well. Fold in sausage mixture and cheese. Generously spray 24 muffin cups with non-stick vegetable spray. Spoon batter into muffin cups, filling 3/4 full. Bake at 375 degrees for about 25 minutes, until golden on both top and bottom. Serve immediately, or wrap in plastic and refrigerate; warm in the microwave. Makes 2 dozen.

Leftover potatoes make scrumptious home fries! In a heavy skillet, heat one to 2 tablespoons oil until sizzling. Add 3 cups cooked, cubed potatoes and 1/2 cup chopped onion. Cook for 5 minutes. Turn potatoes over and season with salt, pepper and paprika. Cook another 5 to 10 minutes, until crisp.

Gram's Bacon & Egg Square Delight

*Sandy Coffey
Cincinnati, OH*

This recipe will feed a crowd at breakfast...it's handy for after-school suppers too! Can be made ahead of time and refrigerated, then popped in the oven. Serve with Texas toast & jelly and a fruit cup for a great quick meal.

10 frozen hashbrown patties, thawed
1 doz. eggs, beaten
1/2 c. milk
1/2 c. sour cream
6 slices bacon, crisply cooked, crumbled and divided

8-oz. pkg. favorite shredded cheese, divided
4 green onions, thinly sliced
1/4 c. red or yellow pepper, finely diced

Spray a 15"x10" jelly-roll pan with non-stick vegetable spray. Crumble hashbrown patties into pan; press in place. Bake, uncovered, at 450 degrees for 15 minutes, or until golden. Meanwhile, in a large bowl, whisk together eggs, milk and sour cream. Stir in half of the bacon and half of the cheese; spread mixture over hashbrowns. Reduce oven to 350 degrees; bake for 15 minutes. Remove from oven; top with remaining bacon and cheese, onions and pepper. Let stand 5 minutes, until cheese melts; cut into squares. Makes 12 servings.

Farmers' markets are open through the fall season, so don't miss out on all the goodies for a harvest breakfast. You'll find fresh eggs, syrup and loads of veggies for a tasty quiche or omelet.

Cheddar-Bacon Quiche

Gladys Kielar
Whitehouse, OH

A tasty breakfast you can put together quickly.

3 eggs
1-1/2 c. milk
1/4 c. butter, melted and cooled
   slightly
1/2 c. biscuit baking mix

pepper to taste
8 slices bacon, crisply cooked
   and crumbled
3/4 c. shredded Cheddar cheese

In a blender, combine eggs, milk and butter. Add biscuit mix and
pepper; process for 15 seconds. Pour into a greased 9" pie plate; top
with bacon and cheese. Bake, uncovered, at 350 degrees for 30 to
35 minutes, until a knife inserted in the center comes out clean. Let
stand 10 minutes; cut into wedges to serve. Makes 8 servings.

Mocha Peppermint Coffee

Courtney Stultz
Weir, KS

This recipe is great for Black Friday shopping. It will give you
a boost on a busy morning and get you in that holiday spirit!

3 c. strong black coffee
1/3 c. vanilla almond milk
1 candy cane, crushed
1 t. baking cocoa

1 t. non-dairy coffee creamer
1 to 2 t. honey
Optional: 1 shot espresso

In a blender, combine all ingredients; process until smooth. Heat until
hot on the stovetop or in the microwave. Pour into coffee cups or large
travel mugs to serve. Serves 2.

Pick up some sturdy vintage mugs at tag sales
for serving hot beverages. They hold the heat
well...wonderful to wrap chilly fingers around!

Koffee Klatch Oatmeal Muffins

Sharon Velenosi
Costa Mesa, CA

Great to serve with coffee for the neighborhood ladies after the kids are off to school. Sometimes I'll use maple sugar for a touch of fall instead of brown sugar.

1 c. long-cooking oats,
    uncooked
1 c. buttermilk
1 c. all-purpose flour
1 t. baking powder
1/2 t. baking soda

1/2 t. salt
1/3 c. butter, softened
1/2 c. brown sugar, packed
1 egg
3/4 to 1 c. raisins

Combine oats and buttermilk in a bowl; let stand for one hour. In a bowl, mix together flour, baking powder, baking soda and salt. In a separate large bowl, whisk together butter, brown sugar and egg. Add flour mixture and oat mixture to butter mixture; stir well but do not overbeat. Fold in raisins. Spoon batter into 12 well-greased muffin cups, filling 2/3 full. Bake at 400 degrees for 20 to 25 minutes. Makes one dozen.

Back-to-school time isn't just for kids. Treat yourself to a class that you've been longing to try...whether it's knitting, cooking, yoga or even a foreign language. Take a girlfriend along for twice the fun!

Happy Apple Pancakes

Kathy Murray-Strunk
Chandler, AZ

I developed this from a basic pancake recipe I've had for years. I call it Happy Apple Pancakes because my family is really happy when I make them! I came up with the syrup recipe one Saturday morning when I was low on maple syrup...it's delicious too.

2 eggs	3 T. sugar
2 c. all-purpose flour	2 T. baking powder
1 c. half-and-half	1 t. salt
1 c. Granny Smith applesauce	3/4 t. cinnamon
1/4 c. extra-light olive oil	1/4 t. allspice

In a bowl, beat eggs with an electric mixer on medium speed until fluffy. Stir in remaining ingredients just until smooth. Pour batter onto a hot griddle over medium-high heat by 1/4 cupfuls. Cook until pancakes are puffed and dry around the edges. Turn and cook other side until golden. Drizzle pancakes with Cream & Sugar Syrup and serve. Makes 16 pancakes.

Cream & Sugar Syrup:

1-1/2 T. butter, sliced	1-1/4 c. brown sugar, packed
1/4 c. half-and-half	1/4 t. vanilla extract

In a saucepan over low heat, melt butter with half-and-half just until starting to bubble. Add brown sugar; stir until completely smooth. Stir in vanilla.

Use a sugar shaker to save clean-up time in the kitchen...it's ideal for dusting powdered sugar onto warm breakfast treats.

Glazed Pumpkin Scones

Donna Wilson
Maryville, TN

I absolutely love pumpkin and scones! These smell so yummy when baking, and taste even better when done. One of my sneaky ways to get kids to eat vegetables.

2 c. all-purpose flour
1/2 c. sugar
1 T. baking powder
1/2 t. salt
1-1/2 t. pumpkin pie spice

1/2 c. butter, diced
1/2 c. canned pumpkin
3 T. milk
1 egg, beaten

Combine flour, sugar, baking powder, salt and spice in a large bowl. Cut in butter with a pastry blender until crumbly; set aside. In a separate bowl, whisk together pumpkin, milk and egg. Fold pumpkin mixture into flour mixture. Form dough into a ball; pat out dough onto a floured surface. Form into a 9-inch circle. Cut into 8 wedges and place on a greased baking sheet. Bake at 425 degrees for 14 to 16 minutes. Drizzle scones with Powdered Sugar Glaze; allow to set. Makes 8 scones.

Powdered Sugar Glaze:

1 c. powdered sugar
2 to 3 T. milk

1/2 t. pumpkin pie spice

Mix all ingredients together, adding enough milk for a drizzling consistency.

Small-town county fairs, food festivals, swap meets...the list goes on & on, so grab a friend and go for good old-fashioned fun. A hearty warm breakfast will get you off to a terrific start.

Stir & Go Biscuits & Sausage Gravy

Pam Hooley
LaGrange, IN

This is a quick, stick-to-your-ribs meal...sometimes I'll even serve it for supper. Since finding this recipe for biscuits made with oil, rather than shortening, I make them more often, and the gravy is so easy to make too.

2 c. all-purpose flour	1 t. salt
2-1/2 t. baking powder	1 c. buttermilk
1/8 t. baking soda	1/2 c. oil
1 t. sugar	Garnish: melted butter

In a large bowl, stir together flour, baking powder, baking soda, sugar and salt. Add buttermilk and oil; stir until moistened. Roll out dough on a floured surface. Cut dough with a biscuit cutter, or drop dough by 1/2 cupfuls, onto an ungreased baking sheet. Bake at 425 degrees for 15 minutes; brush with butter. While biscuits are baking, make Sausage Gravy. Serve gravy over hot biscuits. Serves 4 to 6.

Sausage Gravy:

1 lb. ground pork breakfast sausage	1/2 c. milk
2 T. all-purpose flour	salt and pepper to taste

Brown sausage in a skillet over medium heat. Drain; stir in flour until mixed well. Add milk; cook and stir until thickened. May add more milk to desired consistency. Season with salt and pepper.

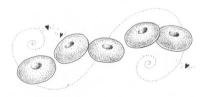

Doughnuts in a dash! Separate refrigerated biscuits and cut out a hole in the center of each. Fry biscuits in hot oil until golden on both sides; drain on paper towels. Roll in sugar and serve warm.

He-Man Breakfast

Melinda Schadler
Fargo, ND

When I was in college, I saw this recipe on the kitchen counter of a family I babysat for. I thought it looked interesting and copied it down. It has now been our family favorite for 25 years! May be assembled the night before and refrigerated. For variety, you can add diced green peppers, mushrooms and other veggies.

32-oz. pkg. frozen shredded or
    diced hashbrowns, divided
2 c. cooked sausage, bacon or
    ham, chopped
1/4 c. onion, chopped
1 c. shredded Cheddar cheese

9 slices pasteurized process
    cheese
1 doz. eggs
1/2 c. milk
salt and pepper to taste

Spread half of frozen hashbrowns on a lightly greased 13"x9" baking pan. (Return remaining hashbrowns to the freezer for another recipe.) Layer with sausage, bacon or ham, onion and cheeses; set aside. Combine eggs, milk, salt and pepper in a blender. Process until well blended; pour over ingredients in pan. Bake, uncovered, at 375 degrees for 35 to 45 minutes, until golden and eggs are set. Serves 6 to 8.

Mmm...maple bacon! Place 12 to 16 thick slices of bacon on a rimmed baking sheet. Bake at 400 degrees for 15 to 20 minutes. Brush bacon with 2 tablespoons of pure maple syrup and return to the oven for 3 to 5 minutes, until crisp and golden. Drain on paper towels...yum!

Jennifer's BBQ Scrambled Eggs

Jennifer Rose Blay
Puyallup, WA

My Dad taught me to put barbecue sauce in scrambled eggs as a special treat. Along with the herbs and spices, the sauce gives these eggs a wonderful flavor. I hope you and your family enjoy this recipe as much as my husband and I do!

8 eggs, beaten
1/4 c. half-and-half
4 t. hickory barbecue sauce
1 t. dried parsley
1/2 t. dried basil
1/2 t. garlic powder
1/2 t. onion powder

1/2 t. celery salt
1/4 t. salt, or to taste
1/4 t. pepper, or to taste
1/8 t. cayenne pepper
1 T. butter
Optional: shredded Cheddar
  cheese

In a large bowl, whisk together eggs, half-and-half, barbecue sauce and seasonings; set aside. Melt butter in a large skillet over medium heat; pour egg mixture into skillet. Scramble eggs over medium-low to medium heat to desired consistency. If desired, sprinkle with shredded cheese just before serving. Makes 4 servings.

Treat yourself to a buttery slice of cinnamon toast. Spread softened butter generously on one side of toasted white bread and sprinkle with cinnamon-sugar. Broil for one to 2 minutes, until bubbly and golden.

Cozy Breakfasts
to Share

Breakfast Burrito Roll-Ups

Angela Murphy
Tempe, AZ

Finger food for breakfast! Use whatever veggies you like.

3 T. green pepper, chopped
1 t. olive oil
3 eggs, beaten
1 T. water

2 8-inch whole-wheat flour
　tortillas
1/2 to 3/4 c. shredded Mexican-
　blend cheese

In a skillet, sauté green pepper in oil until tender. Remove pepper from pan. Whisk together eggs and water; add to hot skillet. Cook until set; do not stir or scramble. Flip to cook the other side. Cut in half; place half of eggs on each tortilla. Top with pepper and cheese; roll up and slice. Serve immediately. Serves one to 2.

Juiced-Up Orange Juice

Wendy Ball
Battle Creek, MI

This is my trick for delicious orange juice at breakfast! I'm often asked what brand of frozen juice I buy. I tell them it's not available in stores and I just smile!

12-oz. can frozen orange juice
　concentrate, thawed

6 to 8 oranges, halved

In a pitcher, prepare orange juice concentrate according to package directions; set aside. With a fruit squeezer or reamer, squeeze juice from oranges into a bowl. Strain pulp, if desired; remove seeds. Add orange juice to pitcher; stir well and chill. Makes 8 servings.

All happiness depends on
a leisurely breakfast.

–John Gunther

19

Cherry Coffee Cake

Tina Goodpasture
Meadowview, VA

I love cherries! As a child, I used to sit in a blackheart cherry tree eating the cherries and spitting out the seeds at my brother below me. Just one of my fondest memories of growing up on a farm in rural Virginia.

12-oz. jar cherry preserves	2 c. biscuit baking mix
1/4 c. brown sugar, packed	2 T. sugar
1/2 c. raisins or chopped nuts	3/4 c. milk
1/4 t. cinnamon	1 egg, beaten

Spread preserves in the bottom of a greased 9"x9" baking pan; set aside. In a small bowl, stir together brown sugar, raisins or nuts and cinnamon; set aside. In a large bowl, combine remaining ingredients. Mix well; beat vigorously for 30 seconds. Spread batter evenly over preserves. Sprinkle with brown sugar mixture. Bake at 400 degrees for 25 to 30 minutes. While still warm, drizzle with Easy Icing. Makes 8 servings.

Easy Icing:

1/2 c. powdered sugar	3/4 t. vanilla extract
1 T. milk or water	

Combine all ingredients; mix until smooth.

Make a gourd garland to hang on the mantel. Choose brightly colored mini gourds with long necks. Tie them onto a length of jute, leaving a few inches of jute between gourds...simple!

Apple & Walnut Scones

Eleanor Dionne
Beverly, MA

These scones are wonderful fresh from the oven with hot tea or coffee. They can also be reheated. Wrap in aluminum foil and place in a preheated 375-degree oven for 5 minutes, then fold back the foil and heat for 3 or 4 more minutes.

2-1/4 c. all-purpose flour
1/2 c. sugar
2 t. baking powder
1/2 t. salt
1/2 c. butter
2 eggs, beaten
1/4 c. milk

2 t. vanilla extract
1 t. lemon zest
1 c. cooking apple, peeled, cored and chopped
1/2 c. chopped walnuts
1/4 c. light brown sugar, packed
1 t. cinnamon

In a large bowl, combine flour, sugar, baking powder and salt; mix well. Cut in butter with 2 knives until crumbly; set aside. In a small bowl, mix eggs, milk, vanilla and lemon zest. Stir into flour mixture; dough will be sticky. Stir in apples. Grease an 11-inch circle on a baking sheet. Place dough on baking sheet; pat into a 9-inch circle. In a small bowl, mix nuts, brown sugar and cinnamon; sprinkle over top. Cut dough into 8 wedges. Bake at 375 degrees for 30 to 35 minutes, until lightly golden. Makes 8 scones.

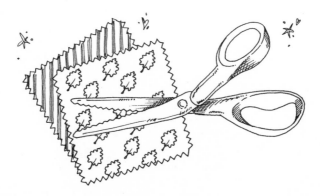

Make a fabric liner for a basket of freshly baked muffins...no sewing required! Use pinking shears to cut an 18-inch square of cotton fabric in a perky fall print. It's so simple, why not make one for the breakfast table and an extra for gift-giving?

Blueberry-Zucchini Muffins

Lynnette Jones
East Flat Rock, NC

These muffins are even better the second day because they become more moist after they sit overnight. So make them when you aren't too busy and they are ready for breakfast or lunchboxes. If you don't have fresh rosemary, leave it out...don't be tempted to use dried rosemary. They are still delicious without the rosemary.

2 c. all-purpose flour	1/4 c. milk
2 t. baking powder	2 eggs, beaten
1/2 t. baking soda	zest and juice of 1 lemon
1/2 t. salt	1-1/2 c. zucchini, grated
1/4 t. nutmeg	1/2 c. blueberries
2/3 c. sugar	3/4 t. fresh rosemary, finely
1/2 c. oil	chopped

Combine flour, baking powder, baking soda, salt and nutmeg in a large bowl; set aside. In a separate bowl, mix together sugar, oil, milk, eggs, lemon zest and juice, zucchini, blueberries and rosemary. Add sugar mixture to flour mixture. Stir just until blended, being careful not to overmix. Spray 12 muffin cups with non-stick vegetable spray or line with paper liners. Fill each cup about 3/4 full of batter. Bake at 400 degrees for 15 to 18 minutes, until golden. Makes one dozen.

Serve fuss-free favorites like Blueberry-Zucchini Muffins... ideal for tailgating Saturday morning. Everyone can easily help themselves while the day's fun is beginning.

Yogurt Parfaits in a Jar

Linda Payne
Snow Hill, MD

Everyone who's tried this recipe thinks they are eating dessert for breakfast...what could be better! In the summertime I try to freeze as much fresh fruit as possible and this is a great use for it.

4 5-oz. containers flavored
    Greek yogurt
1-1/3 c. old-fashioned oats,
    uncooked
2/3 c. milk

4 ripe bananas, sliced
1 c. frozen mixed blueberries,
    strawberries and/or
    other fruit

Combine yogurt, oats and milk in a bowl; stir well. Layer as follows in each of 4 one-pint canning jars: a layer of yogurt mixture, 1/2 sliced banana and a little frozen fruit. Repeat layers. Cover and refrigerate overnight to allow oats to soften. Makes 4 servings.

Make school-day breakfasts fun! Cut the centers from a slice of toast with a cookie cutter, serve milk or juice with twisty straws or put a smiley face on a bagel using raisins and cream cheese.

Cheesy Bacon Brunch Bake

Liz Blackstone
Racine, WI

So cheesy and good! This is my go-to recipe for brunch get-togethers from Thanksgiving to Christmas. It can even be made overnight... just add an extra 1/2 cup milk to the recipe, then cover and refrigerate to bake in the morning.

8 slices bacon
1 c. onion, chopped
1 loaf Italian bread, cubed
   and divided
2 c. shredded Cheddar cheese,
   divided
1 c. shredded mozzarella cheese,
   divided

1 c. cottage cheese
5 eggs, beaten
1-1/2 c. milk
2 t. dry mustard
1/2 t. nutmeg
1 t. pepper

Cook bacon in a large skillet over medium heat until crisp. Remove bacon to paper towels; reserve 2 tablespoons drippings in skillet. Add onion to drippings. Cook and and stir until softened; drain. Spread half of the bread cubes in a lightly greased 13"x9" baking pan. Layer with half each of onion, crumbled bacon, Cheddar cheese and mozzarella cheese. Spread cottage cheese evenly over top. Repeat layering with remaining bread, onion, bacon, Cheddar cheese and mozzarella cheese. Set aside. In a large bowl; whisk together remaining ingredients. Gradually pour egg mixture over cheese layer. Let stand 10 minutes. Bake, uncovered, at 350 degrees for 40 to 50 minutes, until center is set and top is golden. Cut into squares. Makes 12 servings.

Leftover mashed potatoes make tasty breakfast potato pancakes. Combine 2 cups mashed potatoes with one egg and one tablespoon all-purpose flour. Shape into flat patties and pan-fry in 3 to 4 tablespoons melted butter, until golden on both sides.

Brown Sugar Muffins

Helen McKay
Edmond, OK

I used to get these muffins in the cafeteria when I was in college. I loved them so much, the lady who made them for the cafeteria shared this recipe with me. I still love them after 40 years!

1 c. brown sugar, packed	2 c. all-purpose flour
1/2 c. shortening	1 t. baking soda
1 c. milk	1/4 t. salt
1 egg, beaten	1 t. vanilla extract

Combine all ingredients in a large bowl; mix together well. Pour batter into 12 greased muffin cups, filling 2/3 full. Bake at 350 degrees for 30 minutes. Makes one dozen.

My birthday is October 28th, and every year my mom would make it special for me. After all, that's what moms do! The year I turned seven, my mom had planned an after-school birthday party for me and some friends. I came home to find our house decorated all in Halloween pumpkins, black cats, witches, you name it. The best, most memorable part was that my mom had made all the decorations by hand, and in the sweet style I loved...nothing scary for me on Halloween! To a seven-year-old, this was a big deal. I will never, ever forget all the time and creativity she put into that birthday party, from the decorations to the food, and the birthday cake in all its beautiful fall colors. It's a day I'll always remember and a memory I'll always cherish.

–Cindy vonHentschel, Albuquerque, NM

Fiesta Sausage & Egg Casserole

*Wendy Ball
Battle Creek, MI*

An easy overnight breakfast that everyone loves. Or put it together in the morning, then bake later in the day...who says you can't take a breakfast casserole to a potluck dinner?

1 lb. mild chorizo pork sausage,
   casings removed
6 6-inch corn tortillas, sliced
   into 1/2-inch strips and
   divided
12 slices American cheese,
   divided
4-oz. can chopped green chiles,
   drained

8 eggs
1/2 c. half-and-half or milk
1/2 t. chili powder
1/2 t. garlic powder
1/2 t. ground cumin
2 to 3 tomatoes, cut into
   6 slices each
Garnish: sour cream, guacamole

Crumble and cook sausage in a large skillet over medium heat until no longer pink; drain. In a greased 13"x9" baking pan, layer half each of the tortilla strips and sausage; arrange 6 cheese slices on top. Repeat layering with remaining tortilla strips, sausage and cheese slices. Spread evenly with chiles and set aside. In a large bowl, whisk together eggs, half-and-half or milk and seasonings; mix well. Pour over cheese layer; arrange tomato slices on top. Cover and refrigerate for at least 2 hours to overnight. Bake, uncovered, at 350 degrees for 40 to 50 minutes, until center is set and edges are lightly golden. Let stand for about 5 minutes. Cut into squares; serve with sour cream and guacamole. Make 12 servings.

Spoon individual servings of a savory egg casserole into toasty bread bowls. Cut the tops off round crusty bread loaves, hollow them out and brush with olive oil. Pop the bowls into a 400-degree oven for 5 to 10 minutes, until crisp and golden.

Overnight Baked Stuffed Eggs   *Vickie*

A delicious egg casserole that's a snap to make. I like to stir up some muffin batter while the casserole is coming to room temperature, then pop both in the oven together.

8 eggs, hard-boiled and peeled
1 c. plus 3 T. sour cream, divided
2 t. mustard
1/2 t. salt
1/2 c. onion, chopped

2 T. butter
10-3/4 oz. can cream of mushroom soup
1/2 c. shredded Cheddar cheese
Garnish: paprika

Slice eggs in half lengthwise; remove yolks to a bowl and set whites aside. Mash yolks with a fork. Add 3 tablespoons sour cream, mustard and salt; mix well. Spoon mixture into egg whites; set aside. In a saucepan over medium heat, sauté onion in butter until tender. Add soup and remaining sour cream; blend well. Spread half of soup mixture in a greased shallow 3-quart casserole dish. Arrange filled eggs over soup mixture. Spoon remaining soup mixture evenly over eggs. Top with cheese and a dusting of paprika. Cover and refrigerate overnight. Let stand at room temperature 30 minutes before baking. Bake, uncovered, at 350 degrees for 25 to 30 minutes, until bubbly and heated through. Makes 8 servings.

For a sweet change, try an old farmhouse tradition...
a big slice of apple or pumpkin pie for breakfast!

Pumpkin French Toast Bake

Audra Vanhorn-Sorey
Columbia, NC

This recipe is delightful on a cool fall morning. Just pull it from the fridge and bake...the delicious aroma will bring everyone to the breakfast table!

1 loaf crusty French bread, cubed
7 eggs, beaten
2 c. milk
1/2 c. canned pumpkin
2 t. pumpkin pie spice, divided
1 t. vanilla extract
3-1/2 T. brown sugar, packed
Optional: 1/2 c. chopped pecans
Garnish: maple syrup

Spread bread cubes in a greased 13"x9" baking pan; set aside. In a large bowl, whisk together eggs, milk, pumpkin, 1-1/2 teaspoons spice and vanilla. Pour evenly over bread; press down with spoon until bread is saturated. Cover and refrigerate overnight. In the morning, uncover and top with brown sugar, remaining spice and pecans, if desired. Bake, uncovered, at 350 degrees for 35 to 45 minutes, until golden. Serve with maple syrup. Serves 10.

Greet guests with a harvest wreath on the front door. To a straw wreath, hot-glue sunflower heads and mini gourds just for fun. Tie on a big bow of homespun fabric and it's ready to display.

Buckwheat Hotcakes

Kathy Grashoff
Fort Wayne, IN

Hearty full-flavored pancakes to start you off on a sunny fall morning! I like to combine the dry ingredients in a canning jar to give as a gift, tying on a copy of the recipe and a small bottle of maple syrup.

1 c. buckwheat flour	1/2 t. salt
1/4 c. all-purpose flour	2 eggs, beaten
1/4 c. yellow cornmeal	1-1/2 c. buttermilk
1 t. baking powder	2 T. honey
1/4 t. baking soda	1 T. oil

In a large bowl, stir together flours, cornmeal, baking powder, baking soda and salt; set aside. In a separate bowl, whisk together remaining ingredients. Add egg mixture to flour mixture; stir just until blended but still slightly lumpy. For each hotcake, pour 1/3 cup batter onto a hot, lightly greased griddle or heavy skillet. Cook over medium heat for one to 2 minutes per side, until golden, flipping to cook the second side when surface is bubbly and edges are dry. Makes 6 to 8 hotcakes.

There were great farmers' markets in North Carolina where I grew up. I should know, because for three generations, my father's family had a stall at the western North Carolina farmers' market. Every Halloween, in the late afternoon my dad and I made a special trip to a market, just us two. He always let me pick out the pumpkin we took home to carve for our Jack-o'-Lantern. He bought some apple cider to share too and we spent some time just walking around together. Even as a teenager I looked forward to my time alone with Dad to walk and talk on a perfect fall afternoon.

–Angie Fletcher, Katy, TX

Freezer Breakfast Burritos

Connie Hilty
Pearland, TX

These yummy burritos can't be beat for tempting picky eaters before they head off to school.

1 lb. ground pork breakfast
   sausage
1 doz. eggs
salt and pepper to taste
2 T. butter

1/2 c. chunky salsa
2 c. shredded Mexican-blend
   cheese
24 10-inch flour tortillas,
   warmed

In a skillet over medium-high heat, cook sausage until browned. Drain well; set aside sausage and wipe out skillet. Beat eggs in a large bowl; season with salt and pepper. Melt butter in skillet over medium heat. Cook eggs, stirring often, just until scrambled and set. Add cooked sausage and salsa to egg mixture; stir gently. Spoon 1/2 cup egg mixture onto each tortilla; top with one tablespoon cheese. Fold in the ends of each tortilla and roll up, burrito-style. Place burritos on a wax paper-lined baking sheet; freeze until solid. Wrap individually in plastic wrap; pack in plastic zipping bags and return to freezer. To serve, remove plastic wrap; wrap frozen burrito loosely in a paper towel. Microwave on high for one to 3 minutes, until hot and cheese is melted. May also thaw overnight in the refrigerator. Wrap in aluminum foil; bake at 350 degrees for 10 to 15 minutes. Makes 2 dozen.

If you're hosting a sleep-over, the kids will likely stay up late giggling. Plan to serve a mini breakfast at midnight! Set up a room filled with games, movies and lots of yummy things to eat...bagels, muffins and doughnuts.

Cozy Breakfasts
to Share

Quick & Gooey Cinnamon Roll-Ups

Kate Parks
Kettering, OH

These are so perfect on a cool fall morning! My husband and children adore these and they are so quick & easy to put together at the last minute. They're wonderful served alongside a tall glass of chocolate milk for the little ones or a cup of hot tea or coffee for the grown-ups. My little secret...they're delicious topped with ice cream for dessert too!

1 c. sugar	16 marshmallows
2 t. cinnamon, or to taste	2 8-oz. tubes refrigerated
1/2 c. butter, melted	crescent rolls

Combine sugar and cinnamon in a shallow bowl; place melted butter in another shallow bowl. For each roll-up, coat a marshmallow in melted butter, then in cinnamon-sugar. Place marshmallow at the end of a crescent roll and roll up. Fold in ends; pinch seams to close. Dip again in melted butter and coat in cinnamon-sugar. Place roll-ups on a parchment paper-lined baking sheet. Bake at 350 degrees for 10 to 12 minutes, until crisp and golden. Makes 8 servings, 2 roll-ups each.

During the first week of school, deliver a tray of your favorite breakfast goodies to the teachers' lounge... it's sure to be appreciated!

Pumpkin Breakfast Cookies

Leona Krivda
Belle Vernon, PA

These are great for starting off the day with a cup of hot coffee or tea...yummy for snacking too. This makes a good-size cookie. If you want them smaller, just use a smaller scoop and don't bake as long.

1/4 c. coconut oil
1/4 c. honey
1 c. long-cooking oats, uncooked
1 c. quick-cooking oats, uncooked
2/3 c. dried cranberries

2/3 c. pumpkin seeds
1/4 c. ground flax seed
1 t. pumpkin pie spice
1/2 t. salt
1/2 c. canned pumpkin
2 eggs, beaten

Combine coconut oil with honey in a small bowl; microwave just until melted and set aside. In a large bowl, combine all oats, cranberries, pumpkin seeds, flax seed, spice and salt; stir to mix. Add pumpkin, eggs and warm coconut oil mixture; stir until well blended. Drop dough by 1/4-cup scoops onto a parchment paper-lined cookie sheet. Flatten each scoop (cookies will not spread). Bake at 325 degrees for 15 to 20 minutes, until edges are golden. Cool cookies on baking sheet; remove to an airtight container. Makes one dozen.

Save a few seeds from this year's Jack-o'-Lantern to air-dry and tuck into an envelope. Next spring, you and your children can share the fun of planting the seeds and watching them grow into next fall's pumpkins.

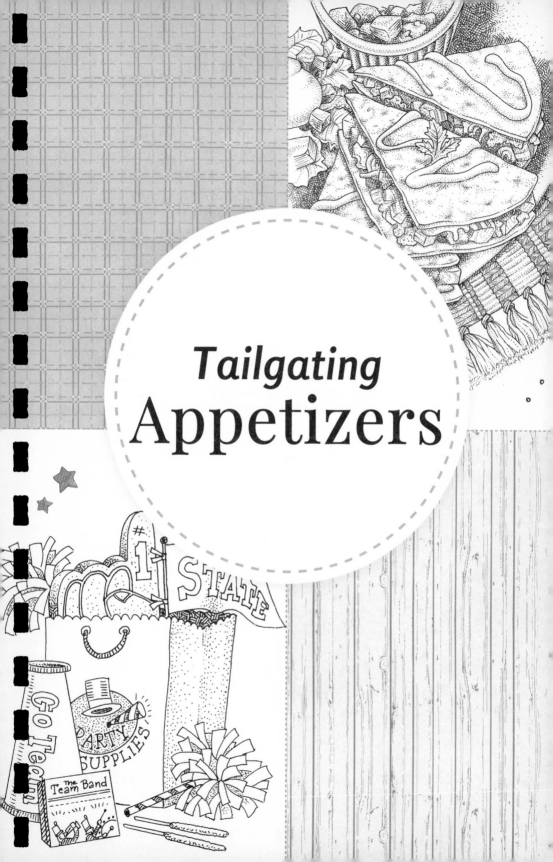

Tailgating
Appetizers

Pork & Apple Bites

Lynn Williams
Muncie, IN

*We love party meatballs, but I was looking for something
a little different. Perfect for a fall tailgating party!*

1 lb. ground pork
1/4 t. cinnamon
1 t. salt
1/8 t. pepper
1/2 c. Granny Smith apple,
    peeled, cored and grated

1/4 c. soft rye bread crumbs
1/4 c. chopped walnuts
1/2 c. water
1/2 c. apple jelly

In a large bowl; combine pork and seasonings; mix well. Add apple,
bread crumbs and walnuts; mix gently until well blended. Form
mixture into balls by tablespoonfuls. Working in batches, brown
meatballs in a large skillet over medium heat. Drain; return all meatballs
to skillet. Pour water into skillet; cover tightly. Cook over medium-low
heat for 15 minutes, or until meatballs are no longer pink in the center.
Remove meatballs to a serving bowl; cover and set aside. Stir apple
jelly into drippings in skillet; cook and stir until jelly is melted. Spoon
sauce over meatballs. Makes about 3 dozen.

Greet visitors with a bountiful farmstyle display on the
front porch. Set a bale of hay in front of a shock of dried
cornstalks, then heap the bale with brightly colored pumpkins,
squash and kale. Add a pot or two of mums and you're done!

Parmesan-Zucchini Bites

Teri Lindquist
Gurnee, IL

These are bursting with flavor! This recipe has been in my collection for years...we love it any time of year. It's a great appetizer and also makes a wonderful side with dinner. They freeze well too.

1.35-oz. golden onion soup mix
1-1/2 c. zucchini, grated
1 c. shredded Swiss cheese
4 eggs, beaten

1/4 c. dry bread crumbs
2 T. grated Parmesan cheese
3/4 t. dried basil

Combine all ingredients in a large bowl. Spoon mixture into 24 well-greased mini muffin pans, filling 2/3 full. Bake at 350 degrees for 20 minutes, or until a toothpick comes out clean. Cool before serving. Makes 2 dozen.

For an easy yet elegant appetizer, try a cheese platter. Choose a soft cheese, a hard cheese and a semi-soft or crumbly cheese. Add a basket of crisp crackers, crusty baguette slices and some sliced apples or pears. So simple, yet sure to please!

Halftime Hoagie Dip

Cyndy DeStefano
Mercer, PA

This is an easy snack that goes a long way for a bunch of hungry boys! The night before my son's high school football games, we like to invite the team over for Big Red Snack Night. This recipe is a favorite served with chips or spread on bread like a sandwich. You can change up the flavor with any deli meats you like.

1/4 lb. deli salami, chopped
1/4 lb. deli roast turkey,
   chopped
1/4 lb. deli baked ham, chopped
1/4 lb. provolone cheese, diced
1 onion, chopped
1 head lettuce, shredded
1 to 2 tomatoes, chopped

1/2 c. mayonnaise
1 t. dried oregano
1/4 t. red pepper flakes
pepperoncini peppers to taste
1 T. olive oil
hoagie rolls or scoop-type corn
   chips

Combine all ingredients except rolls or corn chips in a large bowl; stir well. For the best flavor, cover and refrigerate at least 2 hours, or until serving time, to blend all the flavors. Serve spread on hoagie rolls or with corn chips for dipping. Serves 8.

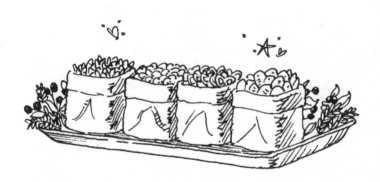

For party snacking, roll down the tops of lunch-size paper bags. Fill with chips and crunchy treats, then set on a tray. Guests can help themselves easily.

Oktoberfest Ale Fondue

Angie Biggin
Lyons, IL

A cheesy, delicious fondue that's fun to share with friends.

3 8-oz. pkgs. shredded
    Monterey Jack cheese
1/4 c. all-purpose flour
12-oz. bottle dark ale or 1-1/2 c.
    beef broth

1 bunch fresh parsley, chopped
1 t. red pepper flakes
salt and pepper to taste
pretzel rods or party rye
    bread slices

Place cheese and flour in a large bowl; toss to combine and set aside.
Pour ale into a saucepan over medium-low heat; bring just to a boil.
Add one cup cheese mixture; stir constantly until cheese is melted.
Add remaining cheese, one cup at a time; stir well. Stir in parsley and
seasonings. Transfer fondue to a fondue pot; broil until golden on top.
Serve hot with pretzel rods or party rye for dipping. Serves 10 to 12.

Cherry tomatoes make yummy party nibbles. Cut off the top of
each tomato, scoop out seeds with a small spoon and turn over
to drain on paper towels. Fill with a favorite creamy dip and
sprinkle with chopped fresh parsley.

Apricot-Apple Cider

Christine Fenner
Prescott Valley, AZ

Great for the fall season!

1 gal. apple cider
11-1/2 oz. can apricot nectar
2 c. sugar
2 c. orange juice
3/4 c. lemon juice

4 3-inch cinnamon sticks
2 t. allspice
1 t. ground cloves
1/2 t. nutmeg

Combine all ingredients in a Dutch oven or soup pot. Bring to a boil over high heat. Reduce heat to medium-low; simmer for 10 minutes. Remove cinnamon sticks; serve hot. Makes about 21 cups.

I was in foster care from the age of three until I turned 18. I spent five years with one special family that left a lasting impression on me and shaped me into the person I am today. Those few short years were the best of my childhood! I can still remember every fall like it was yesterday...the clean, crisp autumn smell in the air, carving pumpkins in the backyard, drinking hot cocoa and watching Charlie Brown and the Great Pumpkin after trick-or-treating. But my favorite of all these memories is of walking into that farmhouse kitchen, seeing cookbooks open, smelling chili simmering and, if I was lucky, warm pumpkin pie in the oven. Even though I wasn't with this family long, the love they showed me was enough to last a lifetime. After having three children of my own I still carry on these traditions. Every year that cool breeze takes me back to a wonderful time in my life that I will hold in my heart forever.

–Jessica Shrout, Owingsville, KY

Sweet Caramel Apple Dip

Ramona Storm
Gardner, IL

This sweet dip is a must when I have my family over for supper after Halloween trick-or-treating. It can be made ahead and stored in an appetizer-size slow cooker and heated before serving.

1/2 c. butter, sliced
3/4 c. brown sugar, packed
14-oz. can sweetened
   condensed milk

1/4 c. light corn syrup
1 t. vanilla extract
apple slices

In a saucepan, melt butter over medium heat. Stir in brown sugar, condensed milk and corn syrup. Bring to a boil; boil for one minute, stirring constantly. Remove from heat; stir in vanilla. Serve warm with apple slices for dipping. Serves 8.

Cranberry Spread

Cathy Miller
Benton, AR

This is delicious as a spread on crackers. It also transforms a turkey sandwich from OK to out-of-this-world! Top one slice of bread with mayo and the other with this spread. Yummy, yet so simple!

2 8-oz. pkgs. cream cheese,
   softened

6-oz. pkg. dried cranberries
snack crackers

Place cream cheese in a serving bowl. Mash with a fork until smooth and creamy. Stir in cranberries; mix well. Cover and refrigerate for 2 hours to overnight, until cranberries have softened. Serve with crackers. Serves 12.

Have an appetizer swap with friends! Each makes a big batch of their favorite dip, spread or finger food, then get together to sample and divide 'em up. You'll all have a super variety of goodies for parties.

Honey-Mustard Spareribs

Megan Brooks
Antioch, TN

You'll love this lip-smacking sauce that's made from just a few pantry ingredients. Cut the spareribs into single ribs for yummy finger food, or into 4-rib sections for dinner. If the weather is nice, grill the microwaved ribs over hot coals instead of broiling.

1/2 c. teriyaki marinade & sauce
2 T. honey
4 t. Dijon mustard
1 t. garlic powder
3 lbs. pork spareribs, cut into serving-size portions

Combine all ingredients except spareribs in a large bowl; mix well. Add spareribs; toss until well coated with sauce. Arrange ribs meat-side up in a microwave-safe glass baking pan; reserve sauce in bowl. Let ribs stand 10 minutes. Cover with plastic wrap. Microwave on medium-high setting for 16 minutes, rotating dish once. Place ribs on a broiler pan; brush with remaining sauce. Place 4 to 5 inches under preheated broiler. Broil for 5 to 6 minutes on each side, brushing once with remaining sauce, until browned. Makes 4 to 6 servings.

The leaves had a wonderful frolic,
They danced to the wind's loud song.
They whirled, and they floated and scampered,
They circled and flew along.

–Anonymous

Appetizers

Spinach & Feta Triangles

Janae Mallonee
Marlborough, MA

*This was one of the first big projects my daughter Meredith took on
in the kitchen. She loves spinach and feta cheese and wanted
to recreate some little treats she had enjoyed in the past.*

3 eggs, divided
1 T. water
10-oz. pkg. frozen chopped
   spinach, thawed and pressed
   dry

1 c. crumbled feta cheese
1 onion, finely chopped
1 sheet frozen phyllo dough,
   thawed

Whisk together one egg and water in a cup; set aside. In a bowl, mix
remaining eggs, spinach, cheese and and onion; set aside. Gently roll
out dough on a floured surface; cut into 12 squares. Spoon spinach
mixture evenly into the center of each square. Fold into triangles; press
edges to seal. Brush egg mixture over triangles. Place triangles on a
greased baking sheet. Bake at 400 degrees for 15 minutes, or until
golden. Makes one dozen.

The high school grandstand is always full for the Friday night
football game, so cheer on your team! A thermos of warm cider
is sure to keep you warm and toasty.

Crunchy Chicken Rolls

Amy Coats
Savannah, MO

This recipe is always a hit with family & friends. I got this recipe in high school cooking class and have been using it ever since! For variety, I sometimes like to replace the plain cream cheese with the garlic & herb kind.

12-oz. can chicken, drained and flaked
2 8-oz. pkgs. cream cheese, softened
3 T. fresh chives, chopped

2 8-oz. tubes refrigerated crescent rolls
2 T. butter, melted
4 c. chicken stuffing mix

In a large bowl, combine chicken, cream cheese and chives; blend well and set aside. Separate and flatten crescent rolls; top each triangle with one tablespoon of chicken mixture. Roll up triangles, sealing well. Dip each triangle into melted butter, then into stuffing mix. Place rolls on a sprayed baking sheet, stuffing-side up. Bake at 350 degrees for 10 to 15 minutes, until lightly golden. Makes 6 to 8 servings. Makes 16 rolls.

Create a creepy "mist" that drifts out of a carved pumpkin face. Just place a can inside a large carved pumpkin, then fill the can halfway with hot water. Wearing gloves, gently drop a piece of dry ice into water.

Blue Cheese-Stuffed Celery

Donna Wilson
Maryville, TN

I tried this recipe a few years back for our Thanksgiving appetizer to keep the kids fed before the big meal. It was amazing...a nice change from plain old cream cheese or peanut butter-filled celery sticks!

6-oz. pkg. crumbled blue cheese
1/2 c. cream cheese, softened
3 T. milk

10 celery stalks, cut into
3-inch sticks
Optional: chopped fresh chives

Combine cheeses and milk in a bowl. Beat with an electric mixer on medium-low speed until well blended. Transfer cheese mixture to a plastic zipping bag; snip off one corner of bag and squeeze into celery sticks. Sprinkle with chives, if desired. Serves 12.

Easiest-ever sandwiches for a get-together...a big platter of cold cuts and cheese, a basket of fresh breads and a choice of condiments so guests can make their own. For the prettiest spread, line the platter with ruffled lettuce, then roll up the sliced cold cuts and stack them.

Chili Powder Cheese Ball

Pat Beach
Fisherville, KY

This cheese ball is one of our all-time family favorites...truly a delicious and unique recipe! My granddaughter has a nut allergy and it can be very difficult to find a recipe that is safe for her, yet everyone else enjoys too. This recipe is a hit with all!

8-oz. pkg. cream cheese, room
    temperature
8-oz. pkg. shredded sharp
    Cheddar cheese

6 T. onion, finely chopped
2 T. mayonnaise
chili powder to taste
snack crackers

In a bowl, combine cheeses, onion and mayonnaise. Mix well with your hands until evenly blended. Form into a ball and place on a serving plate. Sprinkle cheese ball generously with chili powder. Cover with plastic wrap; chill until serving time. Serve with crackers. Serves 8 to 10.

For tasty fun at your next game-day party, turn any favorite cheese ball recipe into a football. Just shape, sprinkle with paprika and pipe on sour cream or cream cheese "laces"...so easy!

Parmesan-Stuffed Mushrooms

*Janae Mallonee
Marlborough, MA*

These savory mushrooms are a favorite dish at my house. Sometimes we even enjoy them as a meal with a crisp tossed salad on the side.

1 lb. whole mushrooms
1/4 c. butter, melted
1/2 c. Italian-flavored dry bread
   crumbs

1/4 c. grated Parmesan cheese
1/2 t. garlic powder
1/2 t. Italian seasoning

Remove stems from mushrooms; dice stems finely and place in a bowl. Add remaining ingredients; mix well and stuff into mushroom caps. Arrange mushrooms in a lightly greased 13"x9" baking pan. Bake, uncovered, at 350 degrees for 15 to 20 minutes, until golden and visibly cooked through. Serves 6 to 8.

Treat yourself to a jolly Jack-o'-Lantern shake! Add 3 scoops vanilla ice cream, 2 tablespoons canned pumpkin, 1/4 cup milk and 1/4 teaspoon pumpkin pie spice to a blender. Blend until smooth. Pour into 2 tall glasses and share with a friend.

Skinny Buffalo Chicken Dip

Stephanie Dardani-D'Esposito
Ravena, NY

I created this recipe because I love buffalo chicken wings, but I do not love all the calories in them. This dip is low on carbs and fat, but high on taste!

2 boneless, skinless chicken
    breasts, cooked and diced
1 c. red-hot buffalo wing sauce
1 c. low-fat blue cheese salad
    dressing

1 c. shredded reduced-fat
    Cheddar cheese
1/3 c. crumbled reduced-fat
    blue cheese
Garnish: celery sticks

Place chicken to a large bowl. Add wing sauce, salad dressing, blue cheese and Cheddar cheese; mix well. Spread in an ungreased 2-quart casserole dish. Bake, uncovered, at 350 degrees for 20 to 25 minutes, until hot and bubbly. Serve with celery sticks. Makes 8 servings.

Serve beverages in old-fashioned Mason jars. Setting the jars inside wire drink carriers makes it easy to tote them from kitchen to harvest table.

Appetizers

Crab-Artichoke Spread

Shirley Howie
Foxboro, MA

This is a low-fat appetizer that tastes great! It is easy to make and is always popular at get-togethers and potlucks.

14-oz. can artichoke hearts,
   drained and chopped
6-oz. can crabmeat, drained
1/3 c. light mayonnaise

1/3 c. non-fat plain yogurt
1/2 t. lemon pepper seasoning
1/2 c. shredded Cheddar cheese
crackers or sliced bread

In an ungreased 1-1/2 quart casserole dish, combine artichokes, crabmeat, mayonnaise, yogurt and seasoning; mix gently. Sprinkle with cheese. Bake, uncovered, at 350 degrees for 25 to 30 minutes, until hot. Serve with crackers or sliced bread. Makes 6 to 8 servings.

Snow Pea & Tomato Appetizer

Janis Parr
Ontario, Canada

Crunchy snow peas combined with juicy tomatoes and a creamy dip makes this fresh-tasting appetizer a big hit with everyone.

3 c. fresh snow peas
2 c. cherry tomatoes
3-oz. pkg. cream cheese,
   softened

1/2 c. sour cream
1/2 t. garlic powder
1/2 t. seasoned salt

Arrange snow peas and tomatoes on a serving plate; cover and chill. In a small bowl, blend remaining ingredients; cover and chill well. At serving time, uncover both and set on buffet table. Serves 12.

Keep extra veggie dippers crisp in the refrigerator by wrapping them in damp paper towels and storing in a plastic zipping bag.

Tasty Fall Cooking

Scarlett's Football Sandwich Ring

Scarlett Hedden
Titusville, FL

When we owned a deli, this was our most-requested sandwich for parties. My husband still requests it every football season. I think it's because the sandwich slices are small enough to hold in his hand. Feel free to add more meat if desired!

2 11-oz. tubes refrigerated
   crusty French loaf
2 t. olive oil
3 cloves garlic, pressed
1/2 t. Italian seasoning
1/3 c. Italian salad dressing
1/3 lb. thinly sliced deli ham
1/4 to 1/3 lb. thinly sliced deli
   turkey
1/4 to 1/3 lb. thinly sliced deli
   roast beef
1/4 lb. sliced American, Swiss or
   Provolone cheese, halved
2 c. romaine lettuce, shredded
1 red onion, thinly sliced
1 green pepper, thinly sliced
1 tomato, thinly sliced
8 pepperoncini peppers

Place both loaves of dough seam-side down on a greased 14" pizza pan, forming one large ring; pinch ends to seal. With a sharp knife, make 8 slashes, 1/2-inch deep, across top of dough. Combine olive oil and garlic; lightly brush over dough. Sprinkle with Italian seasoning. Bake at 350 degrees for 25 to 30 minutes, until golden. Cool bread on pan for 10 minutes; turn out onto a wire rack and cool completely. To assemble, slice bread in half horizontally. Brush cut sides with salad dressing. Layer bottom half with ham, turkey, beef, cheese, lettuce, onion, green pepper and tomato. Add top half of bread; cut into 8 sections. Top each section with a pepperoncini; fasten with a long cocktail pick, if desired. Serve immediately. Makes 8 servings.

Turn the plainest food into a feast with festive trimmings. Pick up table coverings and napkins in team colors at the nearest dollar store and you're halfway to a tailgating party!

Cranberry-Apple Cider

Leona Krivda
Belle Vernon, PA

*I always make this slow-cooker cider for Thanksgiving for
my family. Cider and cranberries makes it feel like fall! Everyone
loves this and it goes well with Thanksgiving desserts.*

4 c. apple cider
4 c. cranberry juice cocktail
2 c. orange juice
1/4 c. sugar, or to taste
1/8 t. ground cloves

3 4-inch cinnamon sticks
Garnish: whole cranberries,
   orange slices, several
   whole cloves

Combine cider, juices, sugar and cloves in a 3-quart slow cooker; stir
well. Add cinnamon sticks. Cover and cook on low setting for 3 to
4 hours. At serving time, garnish with whole cranberries and/or orange
slices studded with whole cloves, as desired. Keep slow cooker set on
low or warm for serving. Recipe may be doubled in a 6-quart slow
cooker. Makes 10 cups.

What's the difference between cider and apple juice? Typically,
cider is raw apple juice that hasn't had the apple pulp filtered
out, for a more robust taste, while apple juice is filtered and
pasteurized, to stay fresh longer. When you can't find cider,
apple juice will work very well. Don't confuse either
with hard cider, which is alcoholic.

Mexican Crescent-Roll Pizza

Karen Wilson
Defiance, OH

This is a great change of pace from the traditional veggie-topped pizza appetizer we all enjoy...everyone loves it! Crescent rolls make this a quick & easy appetizer to toss together.

1 lb. ground beef
1-1/4 oz. pkg. taco seasoning
   mix
1/4 c. water
2 8-oz. tubes refrigerated
   crescent rolls
8-oz. pkg. cream cheese,
   softened

8-oz. container sour cream
4-oz. can sliced black olives,
   drained
1 c. lettuce, shredded
1 tomato, chopped
3/4 c. shredded Cheddar cheese
3/4 c. shredded mozzarella
   cheese

Brown beef in a skillet over medium heat; drain. Stir in taco seasoning and water; simmer for several minutes and remove from heat. Meanwhile, unroll crescent rolls and press into an ungreased 15"x10" jelly-roll pan. Bake at 375 degrees for 10 to 12 minutes, until golden; cool. In a bowl, mix cream cheese and sour cream; spread over cooled crust. Spread beef mixture over cream cheese layer. Sprinkle with olives, lettuce, tomato and cheeses. Cut into squares to serve. Serves 12.

A quick and tasty appetizer in an instant...place a block of cream cheese on a serving plate, spoon sweet-hot pepper jelly over it and serve with crisp crackers or tortilla chips. Works great with spicy salsa or fruit chutney too!

Rancho Taco Dip

Jessica Branch
Colchester, IL

*This is a handy recipe when I have a crowd coming over
or a gathering to attend. It's a nice twist on regular
taco dip and my husband Jeff loves it!*

15-oz. can refried beans
16-oz. container sour cream
1-oz. pkg. ranch salad dressing
   mix
2 c. lettuce, shredded
2 c. shredded Colby Jack cheese
3 green onions, diced

1 tomato, diced
4-1/2 oz. jar diced black olives,
   drained
jalapeño slices to taste
Optional: 1 avocado, halved
   and sliced
tortilla chips

Spread refried beans on a medium platter or pie plate; set aside.
Combine sour cream and dressing mix in a bowl; blend well. Spread
sour cream mixture evenly over beans. Layer with remaining
ingredients except tortilla chips, as desired. Refrigerate for one hour.
Serve with tortilla chips. Serves 8.

A hollowed-out pumpkin is a fun way to serve favorite dips.
Place it on a serving tray, fill it with a scrumptious dip and
surround with a variety of crackers and veggie dippers.

Garlicky Chicken Bites

Megan Brooks
Antioch, TN

Yummy and easy to fix...maybe you should make a double batch!

2 boneless skinless chicken
  breasts, cut into bite-size
  cubes
1/2 c. olive oil

4 cloves garlic, minced
1/4 t. pepper
1/2 c. dry bread crumbs
1/4 t. cayenne pepper

Place chicken in a shallow dish; set aside. In a cup, combine olive oil, garlic and pepper; drizzle over chicken. Turn to coat; cover and refrigerate for 30 minutes. Drain. Combine bread crumbs and cayenne pepper in a separate shallow dish; add chicken cubes and coat well. Arrange on a greased baking sheet in a single layer. Bake at 475 degrees for 10 to 15 minutes, until golden and chicken juices run clear. Makes 4 servings.

Spicy Cranberry Meatballs

Katie Seest
Gastonia, NC

My teen sons enjoy these meatballs in sandwiches, as a snack or even over pasta. They are sweet and spicy.

2 14-oz. cans whole-berry
  cranberry sauce
2 12-oz. jars General Tso's
  sauce

1/2 c. brown sugar, packed
2 26-oz. pkgs. frozen homestyle
  meatballs

Combine sauces and brown sugar in a 5-quart slow cooker; stir to mix well. Add meatballs; stir to coat thoroughly with sauce. Cover and cook on low setting for 4 hours. Makes 12 servings.

Life starts all over again when
it gets crisp in the fall.

–F. Scott Fitzgerald

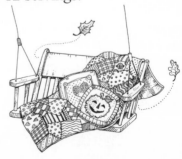

Appetizers

Eileen's Candied Dills

Eileen Bennett
Jenison, MI

No family dinner at my house is complete without a dish of these easy-to-make pickles. The adults love them and our small children are found sneaking spears off the dining room table. These make a great gift packed in a pretty jar...just add a ribbon and a note to keep them refrigerated.

2 24-oz. jars dill pickle spears
   or slices, no garlic, drained
   and juice reserved

1/2 c. tarragon vinegar
2-3/4 c. sugar
2 t. pickling spices

In a large bowl, combine reserved pickle juice with vinegar and sugar; whisk to blend. Tie spices in a cheesecloth bag and add to mixture. Add pickles; let stand at room temperature for 4 hours. Cover and refrigerate for 4 days before serving. If there are any pickles left to store after they have first been served, remove spice bag after one week. Makes one quart.

Note:

If using 3 17-oz. jars dill pickles, use 3/4 cup tarragon vinegar, 3 cups sugar and one tablespoon pickling spices.

Celebrate the spooky season...surround an orange pillar
candle with candy corn in a glass hurricane.

Jalapeño Popper Dip

Lisa Sett
Thousand Oaks, CA

*Great for parties and watching football games! You'll want to
wear a pair of disposable latex gloves when handling the peppers.*

6 to 8 slices bacon, crisply
   cooked and crumbled
2 8-oz. pkgs. cream cheese,
   softened
1 c. shredded Cheddar cheese
1/2 c. shredded mozzarella
   cheese
1 c. mayonnaise

4 to 6 jalapeño peppers, seeded
   and chopped
1/4 c. green onion, diced
1 c. round buttery crackers,
   crushed
1/2 c. grated Parmesan cheese
1/4 c. butter, melted

In a large bowl, combine all ingredients except crackers, Parmesan
cheese and butter. Mix well; transfer to a buttered 2-quart shallow
casserole dish. Combine remaining ingredients in a separate bowl;
sprinkle over the top. Bake, uncovered, at 350 degrees for about
20 to 30 minutes, until hot and bubbly. Serves 10 to 12.

Serve toasty baguette chips with your favorite cheese ball.
Thinly slice a loaf of baguette of French bread. Arrange slices on
a baking sheet and spray lightly with non-stick olive oil spray.
Bake at 350 degrees for 10 minutes, or until crunchy and golden.

Ardena's Salsa

Nancy Christensen
Mission, TX

My sister shared this recipe and it's everyone's favorite. It makes a large amount...perfect for parties!

1 clove garlic
2 28-oz. cans whole tomatoes
1 to 2 4-oz. cans diced jalapeño
   peppers, drained
6-oz. can whole black olives,
   drained and chopped

1 green pepper, chopped
1 red onion, chopped
3 stalks celery, chopped
1 bunch fresh cilantro, chopped
salt to taste

In a food processor, combine garlic and tomatoes with juice; process to desired consistency and transfer to a large bowl. Add remaining ingredients except salt; mix well. Season with salt. Cover and keep refrigerated up to one week. Makes 3 quarts.

Our neighborhood is full of kids and young families. My husband and I spend a lot of time playing outdoors with our boys, so we know most of them. It seemed, though, that many of the other kids didn't know each other, even though they are close in age and go to the same school. Because I love Halloween, I thought it would be a great idea to host a party at our house so everyone could get to know each other. I invited all of the neighbors and their kids over for food, games and fun on Halloween afternoon. I baked up some sugar cookies in Halloween shapes like pumpkins, bats, cats and ghosts. Then I set out the cookies, frosting and Halloween sprinkles at a kid-size table and let the children decorate their own. It was a huge hit! After the party, all of the kids and parents went trick-or-treating together as a group with their new friends.

–Rebecca McKeich, Palm Beach Gardens, FL

Cheesesteak Egg Rolls

Melissa Dattoli
Richmond, VA

One of my most-requested party recipes...everyone loves these! They require some prep but once you get the hang of wrapping them, the process goes quickly. Save time by making the filling a day ahead.

2 c. oil, divided
3/4 lb. deli rare roast beef, thinly
   sliced and finely chopped
1/2 onion, finely chopped

8 to 10 slices provolone cheese,
   cut in half
16 to 20 egg roll wrappers

Heat one tablespoon oil in a skillet over medium-high heat; add beef and onion. Cook, stirring occasionally, until beef is browned and onion is tender. Drain on paper towels; let cool for 10 minutes. May refrigerate if preparing ahead of time. To assemble egg rolls: Place an egg roll wrapper in front of you, in a diamond-shape direction. Place a half-slice of cheese horizontally in the center of the diamond; spoon a heaping 1/4 cup of beef filling over cheese. Set out a small glass of water. Gently lift up the bottom corner of wrapper, over the filling. With a moistened finger, dab a little water on the left and right corners of wrapper; fold each side in over the bottom corner. Dab a little water on the top corner; roll up the egg roll gently but firmly. Dab a little more water on the top corner to keep it closed. Repeat with remaining wrappers and filling. To a large skillet, add 1/2 to one inch remaining oil for frying. Heat over medium-high heat. Fry each egg roll for about 4 minutes per side until golden, adjusting heat as needed. Drain egg rolls on paper towels. Makes 16 to 20.

For tailgating and block parties,
it's fun to serve cold beverages
from a big galvanized tub filled
with lots of ice...looks festive too!

Appetizers

Meatball Sub on a Stick

Mel Chencharick
Julian, PA

These are fun to do! Bring them to a picnic...take them to watch the game with friends. They can be served as a snack or the main dish. You can make your own meatballs, if you like, but the frozen ones are fine and will save you a lot of time.

11-oz. tube refrigerated bread
    sticks, separated
12 10-inch wooden skewers
36 to 48 frozen meatballs,
    thawed

1 c. shredded mozzarella
    cheese
Garnish: warm marinara sauce

Line 2 baking sheets with parchment paper; set aside. Thread a bread stick onto a skewer, starting at end of dough; add a meatball. Forming dough into an S shape around meatballs, alternate dough and meatball 2 to 3 more times, ending with dough. Make sure to spread dough and meatballs away from each other by about 1/4 inch, to allow the dough to expand and the meatballs to bake. Place on baking sheet; repeat with remaining bread sticks and meatballs. Bake at 375 degrees for 20 minutes, or until dough is golden and meatballs are cooked through. Remove from oven; sprinkle each skewer with one to 2 tablespoons shredded cheese. Return to oven for 30 seconds to one minute to melt cheese. Serve immediately with warm marinara sauce. Makes 12 servings.

Stir up some old-fashioned fun this Halloween. Light the house
with spooky candlelight and serve homemade popcorn balls,
pumpkin cookies and hot cider. Bob for apples and play
pin the tail on the black cat...kids of all ages will love it!

Tasty Fall Cooking

Delicious Pull-Apart Pizza Bread

Karen Walker
Brookwood, AL

Our family loves Alabama football and we love our finger foods too. This is a tasty new addition to serve along with other foods we have enjoyed over the years. We love it!

32-oz. pkg. pizza dough
1/3 c. garlic dipping oil
8-oz. pkg. sliced pepperoni
8-oz. pkg. shredded mozzarella
   cheese
1 T. Italian seasoning
1/8 t. dried basil
Garnish: ranch salad dressing,
   garlic butter

Separate pizza dough into small bite-size pieces; place in a large bowl. Drizzle with dipping oil; toss dough pieces to lightly coat. Layer 1/3 of dough pieces in the bottom of a lightly greased Bundt® pan. Layer with half each of pepperoni and cheese; sprinkle with seasonings. Repeat layers, ending with dough pieces. Bake at 375 degrees for 30 to 40 minutes, until bread is golden and cooked through in the center. Remove from oven; invert pan onto a cutting board and turn out bread. To serve, pull bread apart into individual portions. Serve with dipping sauces as desired. Serves 12.

A big pumpkin carved with your house number will lead guests right to your door. Sketch numbers freehand or trace with a stencil, carve them out and slip a votive candle inside...aren't you clever!

Favorite Pub Dip

Susan Church
Holly, MI

*I started making this tasty dip when I still lived at home
and now it reminds me of my family whenever I make it.
A great dip for festive gatherings!*

8-oz. pkg. cream cheese,
   softened
2 5-oz. jars sharp pasteurized
   process cheese spread
1/3 c. beer or beef broth

1 t. Worcestershire sauce
5 drops hot pepper sauce
4 to 6 slices bacon, crisply
   cooked and crumbled
pretzels or crackers

Combine cheeses, beer or beef broth and sauces in a food processor.
Process until smooth; spread in an ungreased 2-quart shallow
casserole dish. Bake, uncovered, at 325 degrees for 20 minutes,
or until hot and bubbly. Stir in bacon. Serve warm with pretzels or
crackers. Serves 6 to 8.

Clever drink stirrers make hot beverages special. Besides
tried & true cinnamon sticks, try cinnamon-flavored
candy sticks, bright-colored rock candy sticks and
sugar cane swizzle sticks.

Batter-Fried Mushrooms

Beverley Williams
San Antonio, TX

*I wanted a tasty appetizer and came up with these
delicious gems. They are the first thing to go at parties!*

1 c. all-purpose flour
1/2 c. cornstarch
1 T. grated Parmesan cheese
3/4 t. baking powder
1/2 t. garlic powder
1/2 t. Italian seasoning
1/2 t. dried thyme
1/8 t. cayenne pepper
1/8 t. salt

1/4 t. pepper
1 c. buttermilk
2 c. panko bread crumbs
10-oz. pkg. cremini mushrooms,
    stems trimmed
oil for frying
Garnish: favorite dipping sauce
    or ranch salad dressing

In a shallow dish, combine flour, cornstarch, Parmesan cheese, baking powder and seasonings; mix well. Add buttermilk; stir to form batter. Place bread crumbs in a separate shallow dish. Dip mushrooms into batter; let excess drip off. Roll mushrooms in bread crumbs to coat. Heat one inch oil in a skillet over medium heat. Working in batches, use tongs to carefully add mushrooms to hot oil; do not crowd the mushrooms. Cook, turning occasionally, for 7 to 10 minutes, until golden. Gently remove mushrooms to a paper towel-lined plate. Allow to cool for 2 to 5 minutes. Serve with dipping sauce or ranch dressing. Serves 4 to 6.

Assemble a Mason jar bouquet in a jiffy! Cut a circle from a plastic net onion bag, stretch it tight and fasten in place with the jar ring. Trim off the excess, then simply poke the flower stems through the net.

Appetizers

Fried Dill Pickle Chips

Beckie Apple
Grannis, AR

A favorite in our house...we love these served with ranch dressing.

1 c. dill pickle chips	3/4 c. seltzer water
1/2 c. all-purpose flour	4 8-inch wooden skewers
2 t. cornmeal	2 c. oil
1-1/2 t. cornstarch	Garnish: ranch salad dressing
1/2 t. seasoned salt	

Drain pickle chips on paper towels. In a bowl, combine flour, cornmeal, cornstarch and salt; mix well. Add seltzer water; stir well. Heat oil in a deep skillet over medium heat. Using skewers, dip pickles into batter to coat. Add pickles to hot oil, 4 to 6 at a time. Turn with skewers until golden; drain on paper towels. Serve with ranch dressing. Serves 4.

Saucy Apricot Kielbasa

Kim Bugaj
Manchester, CT

I have been making this recipe for years now! It is a huge hit at our barbecues and family get-togethers. I have tried other preserves, but we like the apricot best!

12-oz. jar apricot preserves	3 lbs. Kielbasa sausage, halved
1-3/4 c. dark brown sugar,	lengthwise and cut into bite-
packed	size slices
1 c. water	

In a 5-quart slow cooker, combine preserves, brown sugar and water. Stir until combined. Gently fold in Kielbasa slices; stir until well coated. Cover and cook on low setting for about 4 hours. Makes 15 to 20 servings.

Harvest Moon Popcorn

Irene Robinson
Cincinnati, OH

*This is a great snack to have on hand instead of
cereal mix. It's also terrific for lunchboxes.*

8 c. popped popcorn
2 c. canned shoestring potatoes
1/2 c. butter, melted
1 t. Worcestershire sauce
1 t. lemon pepper seasoning

1 t. dried dill weed
1/2 t. onion powder
1/2 t. garlic powder
1/4 t. salt

Combine popcorn and potatoes in a large bowl; set aside. In a separate small bowl, stir together remaining ingredients. Drizzle butter mixture over popcorn mixture; toss to coat. Spread on a rimmed baking sheet. Bake, uncovered, at 350 degrees for 8 to 10 minutes. Cool; store in an airtight container. Makes about 10 cups.

Package homemade goodies like candies, peanut brittle and spiced nuts in snack-sized sacks. Set several in a basket by the door so guests have a yummy treat to take home.

Sue's Firecrackers

Sue Whitley
Lubbock, TX

When I was given a similar recipe, I thought I could improve on it with more seasonings. My new recipe was a big hit! My daughter-in-law and 9-year-old granddaughter are disappointed if I'm out of these zesty crackers. I keep copies of the recipe in my purse all the time as I'm often asked for it.

16-oz. pkg. saltine crackers
1-1/2 c. canola oil
1-oz. pkg. ranch salad dressing
    mix
1 t. garlic powder

1 t. onion powder
1 t. ground chipotle chili pepper
1 t. red pepper flakes
1 t. cayenne pepper
1 t. pepper

Place crackers in a one-gallon plastic zipping bag; set aside. Combine oil and seasonings in a bowl; mix well and pour over crackers. Close bag; turn bag frequently, until oil is absorbed. For the best flavor, make a day before serving. Makes 12 to 15 servings.

My favorite harvest memory is not from my childhood, but from my children's. Every fall we take the kids to a "Punkin Patch" and let them choose their pumpkins. We have a great time looking at all the produce and then picking their favorite pumpkins...sometimes too big to carry! After we get back home, we share warm apple cider and chocolate chip cookies while picking designs to carve into the pumpkins. Sometimes the designs are elaborate, sometimes simple, but we have fun together and that is the best part.

–Tanya Coblentz, Shellsburg, IA

Mom's After-School Snack Mix

Elisha Wiggins
Suwanee, GA

My children love to make this with me for an after-school snack. I let them do all of the measuring and mixing. You can change out any of the ingredients for just about anything you have on hand.

4 c. bite-size crispy cereal
    squares
2 c. bear-shaped graham snack
    crackers
3/4 c. dried cranberries

3/4 c. honey-roasted peanuts
3/4 c. chocolate-covered raisins
1 c. pretzel nuggets
1 c. candy-coated chocolates

Combine all ingredients in a large bowl and toss to mix. Use a measuring cup to divide up mixture into small plastic zipping bags. Makes 8 to 10 servings.

For a clever serving idea, line vintage lunch or trick-or-treat pails with wax paper and fill with easy-to-nibble appetizers, nuts or candies.

Appetizers

Easy Game-Time Snack Mix

Nola Coons
Gooseberry Patch

A last-minute snack...open the containers & toss everything together! For tailgating parties, I like to use candy-coated chocolates in my favorite team's colors.

5 c. bite-size crispy rice cereal
   squares
2 19-oz. pkgs. candy-coated
   chocolates
16-oz. pkgs. mini pretzel twists

16-oz. jar honey-roasted
   peanuts
13.7-oz. pkg. baked white
   cheese snack crackers

Combine all ingedients in a very large bowl. Toss gently to mix well.
Store, covered, in an airtight container. Makes 30 cups.

Give your favorite snacker a giant tin filled with
party mix. Decorate the outside of a large coffee can with
acrylic paint in fun fall designs, leaves, scarecrows,
pumpkins or apples...an irresistible treat!

Caramel Apple Pie Nachos

Coleen Lambert
Luxemburg, WI

My grandkids just love this...they can fix it by themselves!

2 7-oz. pkgs. cinnamon & sugar
   pita chips
21-oz. can apple pie filling

Garnish: caramel ice cream
   topping, whipped cream

Layer pita chips on a serving plate; spoon pie filling over chips. Drizzle with caramel topping; dollop with whipped cream. Serve immediately. Makes 8 servings.

S'mores Nachos

Cassie Hooker
La Porte, TX

A great snack for cool fall evenings. It is quick and simple to make and it is so delicious to eat!

12 graham crackers, coarsely
   broken
1-1/2 c. semi-sweet chocolate
   chips

4 c. mini marshmallows
Optional: additional chocolate
   chips, melted

In an 8"x8" glass baking pan, make layers of graham crackers, chocolate chips and marshmallows. Bake, uncovered, at 350 degrees for 10 to 15 minutes, until marshmallows are golden. Drizzle with melted chocolate chips, if desired. Allow to cool slightly before serving. Serves 6.

Share chills and thrills with a monster movie night. Make a big batch of a favorite snack, let the kids each invite a special friend and scatter plump cushions on the floor for extra seating. Sure to be fun!

Fall
Soup
Suppers

Savory Bacon-Corn Chowder

Betty Gretch
Owendale, MI

My family always requests this during sweet corn season. It is a hearty soup and will warm you up on a cool fall day.

8 slices bacon, cut into
   1-1/2 inch pieces
2 onions, chopped
3 carrots, peeled and minced
2 potatoes, peeled and diced

5 c. chicken broth
16-oz. pkg. frozen corn,
   or 3 c. fresh corn
salt and pepper to taste
1 c. whipping cream

In a large skillet over medium heat, cook bacon until crisp. Remove bacon to a plate with a slotted spoon. Reserve 3 to 4 tablespoons drippings in skillet. Add onions and carrots; sauté until onions are soft and translucent. Add potatoes; sauté for one minute and drain. Add chicken broth, corn and seasonings; bring to a boil. Reduce heat to medium-low. Simmer, partially covered, until potatoes are very tender. Remove 1/3 of soup to a blender; purée until smooth. Combine puréed soup with cream; return to pan. Simmer over low heat until heated through. Stir in reserved bacon; keep warm until ready to serve. Makes 6 servings.

Use raffia to secure cinnamon sticks or tiny ears of Indian corn around a plump pillar candle. Set at each place setting for a seasonal glow.

Fall
Soup Suppers

Easy Bean Stew

Linda Smith
Fountain Hills, AZ

This is a wonderful hearty slow-cooker stew, very tasty yet so simple to make. While living in the midwest, we made it often in the fall and winter...it always seemed to hit the spot! If you use extra-lean beef or turkey like I do, there's no need to brown it first. Mix & match your favorite canned beans as you like.

2 lbs. extra-lean ground beef
    or ground turkey
3 15-oz. cans pinto or kidney
    beans, drained

2 10-3/4 oz. cans tomato soup
10-3/4 oz. can Cheddar cheese
    soup
salt and pepper to taste

Crumble uncooked beef or turkey into a 6-quart slow cooker. Add remaining ingredients; stir well. Cover and cook on low setting for 6 to 8 hours, or on high setting for 3 to 4 hours. Makes 8 to 10 servings.

Invite friends over for a plant swap this fall! Everyone goes home with a new plant and a start on their own friendship garden. Keep the menu easy...ask friends to tote along their favorite slow-cooker soup with the recipe for sharing.

Beefy Vegetable Soup

Cynthia Johnson
Verona, WI

This slow-cooker soup is so easy to put together. It's delicious and makes your home smell wonderful, especially on chilly fall nights!

1 lb. ground beef
1 onion, chopped
1 clove garlic, minced
16-oz. can kidney beans
16-oz. can cannellini beans
10-oz. pkg. frozen corn & pea
    blend

14-1/2 oz. can diced tomatoes
2 8-oz. cans tomato sauce
1 c. carrots, peeled and shredded
1 t. chili powder
1/2 t. dried basil
1/2 t. salt
1/4 t. pepper

In a skillet, cook beef, onion and garlic over medium heat until beef is no longer pink; drain. Transfer to a 5-quart slow cooker. Add remaining ingredients; mix well. Cover and cook on low setting for 8 hours, or until thick and bubbly. Makes 8 servings.

As I am preparing my daughter to go back to school, it takes me back to my favorite school lunch. These days, schools do not serve soup & sandwiches like they did when I went to school. I always looked forward to the chicken noodle soup and bologna sandwich. The special part of the sandwich was the butter and mustard on it. It might seem like a weird combination, but it was so good! Every now & then, I need to make myself one so I can go back to the days when life was a little simpler. I sit and remember coloring a picture for my favorite teacher.

–Michele Coen, Delevan, NY

Soup Suppers

Hearty Squash Soup

Kristin Stone
Little Elm, TX

I love fall...apples, squash, the whole lot! This is the best squash soup ever, and fall is the perfect season for it. To save a little time, substitute 2 cans of pumpkin for the butternut squash. If you prefer a meatless soup, it's almost as good without the bacon.

1 lb. bacon, diced
4 c. reduced-sodium chicken
   broth, divided
3 potatoes, peeled and chopped
2 carrots, peeled and sliced
1 butternut squash, or 2 15-oz.
   cans pumpkin

1 c. fresh or frozen corn
1 to 2 t. Creole seasoning,
   or salt and pepper to taste
1 t. ground cumin
1/2 t. nutmeg

Cook bacon in a large stockpot until crisp; drain and remove to a separate dish. Add 3 cups chicken broth to pot; add potatoes and carrots. Bring to a boil; reduce heat to medium-low and simmer until vegetables are tender, 15 to 20 minutes. Meanwhile, use a fork to pierce several holes in the squash. Microwave squash on high for 10 to 15 minutes, until tender when squeezed, rotating several times while cooking. Peel and remove seeds. Place squash pulp in a blender or food processor with remaining broth; process until smooth. Add to stockpot. Stir in corn and seasonings; simmer until heated through, 5 to 10 minutes. Sprinkle reserved bacon over each serving. Serves 6.

Prewarmed soup bowls are a thoughtful touch. Set oven-safe crocks on a baking sheet and tuck into a warm oven for a few minutes. Ladle in hot, hearty soup...mmm, pass the cornbread!

Best October Reuben Soup

Sandy Coffey
Cincinnati, OH

Great for celebrating Oktoberfest and football games.
Serve with a basket of light and dark rye breads.

1/2 c. beef broth
1/2 c. chicken broth
1/4 c. celery, coarsely chopped
1/4 c. onion, coarsely chopped
1/4 c. green pepper, coarsely
    chopped
1 T. cornstarch
2 T. water

1/4 lb. corned beef, shredded
1 c. baby Swiss cheese, diced
3/4 c. sauerkraut, drained,
    rinsed and squeezed dry
1/4 c. butter
2 c. half-and-half
1/8 t. salt
1/8 t. pepper

Combine broths, celery, onion and green pepper in a medium
saucepan; bring to a boil. Reduce heat to medium-low and simmer
until vegetables are crisp-tender, about 5 minutes. In a cup, dissolve
cornstarch in water. Add to soup; stir well and cook until soup
thickens, about 5 minutes. Remove from heat. Stir in corned beef,
cheese and sauerkraut. In a small saucepan over low heat, melt
butter and blend in half-and-half. Add to soup; stir until smooth and
heated through. Season with salt and pepper. Ladle into bowls.
Makes 8 servings.

oak leaf
maple leaf
pumpkin
scarecrow
red apple

While the soup is simmering, plan a harvest scavenger hunt
for the whole family. Send them out with a list of fall finds...
a golden oak leaf, a russet-red maple leaf, a pumpkin, a scarecrow
and a red apple, just to name a few. It's not only lots of fun, it's
a great way to get outside and enjoy the fabulous fall weather!

Pappy Shaffer's Chili

Marcia Shaffer
Conneaut Lake, PA

My grandkids often ask for this slow-cooker chili when visiting and my husband is happy to make it! Great for tailgating, family get-togethers and chilly nights.

2 lbs. onions, sliced
3 T. butter
3 to 5 lbs. ground beef
32-oz. bottle catsup
4 c. water
3 48-oz. cans kidney beans
2 28-oz. cans tomato sauce

28-oz. can diced tomatoes
3 T. chili sauce
salt and pepper to taste
Optional: jalapeño peppers,
    chopped, with or without
    seeds

In a very large skillet over medium heat, brown onions in butter until well cooked but not browned. Add beef and cook until browned; drain well. Combine onions and beef in a 6 to 7-quart slow cooker. Add catsup; pour water into catsup bottle and add it as well. Stir in remaining ingredients. Jalapeño seeds may be added according to desired heat level. Cover and cook on low setting for 8 hours. Makes 10 to 12 servings.

Make a quick and hearty chili-cornbread casserole. Spread 4 cups of leftover chili in a cast-iron skillet. Mix up a box of corn muffin mix and spread batter over chili. Bake at 400 degrees for 15 to 20 minutes, until cornbread is golden and chili is bubbly. Come & get it!

Spinach Tortellini Soup

Jeanne Koebel
Adirondack, NY

We all get lots of opportunities to overindulge at autumn get-togethers. This quick & easy, healthy, low-cal soup is just what you need, the day after!

1 onion, finely chopped
3 cloves garlic, minced
2 t. olive oil
2 32-oz. containers sodium-free chicken or vegetable broth
1/2 to 1 c. baby carrots, finely chopped
2 t. Italian seasoning
Optional: 1/2 t. salt
1/4 t. pepper

15-oz. can low-salt diced tomatoes, seasoned if desired
16-oz. pkg. frozen tortellini, uncooked
5-oz. pkg. fresh baby spinach, stems trimmed
Optional: grated Parmesan cheese

In a heavy soup pot or Dutch oven over medium heat, sauté onion and garlic in olive oil until translucent. Add broth, carrots and seasonings. Bring to a boil; simmer for about 5 minutes. Add tomatoes and tortellini; return to a boil. Reduce heat to medium-low and simmer for about 10 minutes, until tortellini is cooked. Stir in spinach; simmer until spinach is wilted. Serve with Parmesan cheese sprinkled on top, if desired. Makes 8 servings.

Top bowls of soup with crunchy cheese toasts. Cut bread with a mini cookie cutter and brush lightly with olive oil. Place on a broiler pan and broil for 2 to 3 minutes, until golden. Turn over and sprinkle with freshly shredded Parmesan cheese. Broil another 2 to 3 minutes, until cheese melts.

Sweet Potato Biscuits with Honey Butter

Janet Sharp
Milford, OH

These tender biscuits are delicious served for breakfast, brunch or dinner. Great for using up leftover sweet potatoes, too. The recipe is easy to double and leftovers keep well in the freezer.

1-1/4 c. all-purpose flour
2 T. plus 1 t. sugar
1 T. plus 1 t. baking powder
1/2 t. salt
1 t. cinnamon

1/8 t. nutmeg
1/8 t. allspice
3/4 c. mashed sweet potatoes
1/4 c. butter, melted
2 to 4 T. milk

Line a baking sheet with parchment paper or lightly spray with non-stick vegetable spray; set aside. In a large bowl, sift together flour, sugar, baking powder, salt and spices; mix well. In a separate bowl, stir together sweet potatoes and melted butter; add to flour mixture and stir to combine. Add milk, one tablespoon at a time, until dough is moistened enough to pull away from the bowl. Turn the dough out onto a lightly floured surface or wax paper. Knead 5 to 6 times, until smooth; pat out dough into an 8-inch circle. Using a 2-inch cutter dipped in flour, cut out biscuits, re-rolling scraps once. Place on baking sheet. Bake at 450 degrees for 10 minutes, or until lightly golden. Serve with Honey Butter. Makes 6 biscuits.

Honey Butter:

1/4 c. butter, softened

1 T. honey

Mix butter and honey until well blended. Cover and chill.

Take an autumn bike ride...fill the bike's basket with a thermos of hot soup and a loaf of bread. What fun!

Homemade Tomato Soup

Susan Buetow
Du Quoin, IL

As soon as the weather turns chilly, we love eating tomato soup and grilled cheese sandwiches for lunch. This recipe is so easy that I'm almost embarrassed to share it!

46-oz. can tomato juice
2-3/4 c. milk or water
2 T. butter
1 onion, chopped
1 T. garlic, minced, or garlic
  powder to taste

Optional: hot peppers or kimchi
  to taste
salt and pepper to taste
Garnish: shredded Parmesan
  cheese, saltine crackers

Add tomato juice to a large saucepan. Stir in milk, water or a combination of both. Add onion and garlic or garlic powder. Bring to a boil over medium heat. Reduce heat to low; simmer until onion is soft, about 20 minutes, stirring occasionally. Season with salt and pepper. For a spicier soup, add hot peppers or kimchi just before serving, or let everyone add their own. Serve soup topped with Parmesan cheese and crackers. Makes 8 servings.

My mother always made the best chili. One cold fall day, she whipped up a pot of chili we will never forget. She accidentally used cinnamon instead of chili powder. Instead of telling us, she tried to spoon out as much of the cinnamon as she could and added some extra chili powder. Mom served it up with a smile on her face, hoping we wouldn't notice. It was horrible, but it was a meal we never forgot!

–Julie Owens, Freeville, NY

Fall
Soup Suppers

Autumn Herb Bread

Sharon Velenosi
Costa Mesa, CA

The bread is packed with the flavors of fall! I bake it before Thanksgiving so we can use it for turkey sandwiches. If you don't have these herbs on hand, you can substitute 1-3/4 teaspoons poultry seasoning.

1 env. active dry yeast	3 eggs, beaten
1/4 c. very warm water, 110 to 115 degrees	6 to 7 c. all-purpose flour, divided
1/4 c. sugar or honey, divided	3/4 t. dried thyme
1-1/2 c. warm milk	1 t. dried sage
1 T. salt	3/4 t. dried marjoram
1/2 c. margarine, melted	Garnish: additional milk

In a large bowl, combine yeast, warm water and one tablespoon sugar or honey. Let stand until yeast is softened. Add milk, remaining sugar or honey, milk, salt, margarine, eggs and 2 cups flour to yeast mixture. Mix well. Cover and let rise in a warm place for about one hour, until bubbly. Combine herbs and add to mixture. Stir in enough of remaining flour to make a stiff dough. Knead dough on a floured surface until satiny and elastic. Place in a large greased bowl, turning once to bring greased side up. Cover and let rise in warm place until double in size. Punch down dough and let rise another 10 minutes. Shape dough into 2 loaves; place in 2 greased 9"x5" loaf pans. Brush tops with milk. Let rise for about 45 minutes, until well rounded at center and sides of dough reach the top of the pans. Bake at 375 degrees for 50 minutes, or until a toothpick comes out clean. Makes 2 loaves.

Sticky dough got you stuck? Just spray a rubber spatula with non-stick vegetable spray before scraping the dough from the bowl...it'll slide right out!

Creamy Turkey-Vegetable Soup

Shannon Reents
Bellville, OH

My go-to recipe when I have lots of leftover turkey from the holidays! Leftover mixed veggies can be added too. This soup freezes well..make it now, enjoy it later.

1 onion, finely chopped
2 T. butter
3 c. new redskin potatoes, diced
2 14-1/2 oz. cans chicken broth
2 c. cooked turkey, cubed

2 c. frozen mixed vegetables, thawed
1/2 t. white pepper
1/2 t. poultry seasoning
2 c. whipping cream

In a soup pot over medium heat, sauté onion in butter until tender. Add potatoes and broth; bring to a boil. Reduce heat to medium-low; cover and simmer for 20 minutes. Stir in turkey, vegetables and seasonings. Simmer another 10 to 12 minutes, until vegetables are tender. Stir in cream; heat through without boiling. Makes 8 to 10 servings.

The ultimate comfort food...place a scoop of mashed potatoes in the center of a soup bowl, then ladle hearty soup all around the potatoes.

Fall
Soup Suppers

Spiced Pear Bread

Joyceann Dreibelbis
Wooster, OH

Pears give this bread a delicious taste and help keep it nice and moist. I give family & friends these small loaves year 'round.

2 c. all-purpose flour
1 c. sugar
1 t. baking powder
1/2 t. baking soda
1/4 t. cinnamon
1/2 c. butter

2 eggs
1/4 c. buttermilk
1 t. vanilla extract
1 c. pears, peeled, cored and
    finely chopped

In a large bowl, combine flour, sugar, baking powder, baking soda and cinnamon; mix well. Cut in butter with 2 knives until mixture resembles coarse crumbs. In a small bowl, beat eggs, buttermilk and vanilla; stir into flour mixture just until moistened. Fold in pears. Spoon into 3 greased 5-3/4"x3" mini loaf pans. Bake at 350 degrees for 30 minutes, or until a toothpick inserted near the center comes out clean. Cool in pans 10 minutes before removing to wire racks to cool. Makes 3 mini loaves.

Beer Bread

Sharry Murawski
Oak Forest, IL

I loved making the beer bread mixes sold at home parties, but they sure can be expensive. I pulled together some different recipes to come up with this simple version that tastes just as good!

3 c. self-rising flour
12-oz. bottle regular or non-
    alcoholic beer, room
    temperature

1/3 c. sugar
3 T. butter, melted

In a large bowl, mix flour, beer and sugar. Spoon into a greased 9"x5" loaf pan. Drizzle melted butter over top. Bake at 350 degrees for one hour, or until golden. Makes one loaf.

Scrambled Cheeseburgers

Wendy Meadows
Spring Hill, FL

I've been making this recipe since my kids were little. They did not like traditional hamburgers and this was more to their liking. Now it's a staple on our menu. My son will actually call me to find out what night I am making this so he can come to dinner.

1 lb. ground beef
1/2 to 3/4 c. onion, diced
Optional: garlic powder, salt and
    pepper to taste
4 slices American, Cheddar,
    Pepper Jack or Swiss cheese

4 to 6 hamburger buns, split
Garnish: favorite cheeseburger
    toppings

Add onion to a large skillet over medium heat; crumble in beef. Cook and stir, breaking up any larger pieces, until onion is translucent and beef is no longer pink. Drain. Stir in garlic powder, salt, and pepper, if using. Spread beef mixture into an even layer in skillet. Arrange cheese slices over beef. Once the cheese starts to melt, stir it into the beef. Serve spooned onto buns; garnish with your favorite toppings. Makes 4 to 6 servings.

Serve up mummy dogs in a jiffy...perfect alongside a bowl of chili before trick-or-treating! Simply wrap strips of bread stick dough around hot dogs. Arrange them on an ungreased baking sheet and bake at 375 degrees for 12 to 15 minutes.

Soup Suppers

Pizza Broiled Sandwiches

Marsha Baker
Pioneer, OH

I found this treasured recipe in a cookbook given to me when my children were very young. They grew up on this tasty recipe and now they serve it to their own families. Keeps in the fridge for several days, so it's perfect for busy families. If you like, spread the mixture on hamburger bun halves instead of French bread.

1 lb. ground beef, browned and
    drained
16-oz. pkg. shredded Cheddar or
    Co-Jack cheese
6-oz. can chopped black olives,
    drained

10-3/4 oz. can tomato soup
1/3 c. onion, drained
1/4 c. oil
1/2 t. dried oregano
2 loaves French bread, sliced on
    the diagonal

Brown beef in a skillet over medium heat; drain well. In a large bowl, combine beef and remaining ingredients except bread; mix well. Cover and refrigerate for 4 hours. To serve, spread beef mixture on slices of French bread, making sure to spread mixture all the way to the edges to prevent burning under the broiler. Place slices on a broiler pan; broil until bubbly and golden. Makes 12 to 15 servings.

Bring out Mom's vintage Thanksgiving china early to get into
the mood for fall. Use the bowls for soup suppers, the teacups
for dessert get-togethers and even layer sandwich fixin's
on the turkey platter!

Cajun Okra Gumbo

Betty Kozlowski
Newnan, GA

Mom's Cajun gumbos were a favorite with all eight of us kids. We grew up in New Orleans, but Mom & Dad both came from small Louisiana farming towns, and were both of strong French descent.

16-oz. pkg. frozen okra
1/2 onion, chopped
28-oz. can diced tomatoes
6 to 8 pieces chicken, skin
  removed

1 lb. smoked pork sausage,
  sliced
8 to 10 c. water
salt to taste
cooked rice

Spray a large soup pot with non-stick vegetable spray. Add okra; sauté over medium heat for 5 to 10 minutes. Add onion, tomatoes with juice, chicken, sausage and enough water to fill pot to 2 inches from the top of pot. Bring to a boil; reduce heat to low. Season with salt. Simmer for one hour, stirring occasionally. At serving time, discard chicken bones. Serve gumbo ladled over cooked rice. Makes 8 servings.

For a quick & easy table runner, choose cotton fabric printed with autumn leaves, Indian corn and pumpkins in glowing gold, orange and brown. Simply pink the edges... it will dress up the dinner table all season long!

Soup Suppers

White Chicken Chili

Hannah McCoy
Arbuckle, CA

*So simple to make! This hearty chili is extra delicious
with fresh lime juice squeezed on top.*

10-oz. can diced tomatoes with
  green chiles
15-oz. can corn
2 boneless, skinless chicken
  breasts, cooked and
  shredded
16-oz. can black beans, drained
  and rinsed

1-oz. pkg. ranch salad dressing
  mix
1 t. chili powder
1 t. onion powder
8-oz. pkg. cream cheese, cubed
cooked rice

In a large saucepan, combine undrained tomatoes, undrained corn and
remaining ingredients except rice. Cook over medium-low heat, stirring
occasionally, until heated through and cream cheese melts. Serve chili
ladled over cooked rice. Makes 4 to 6 servings.

A quick fall craft for kids...hot glue large acorn caps
onto round magnets for whimsical fridge magnets.

Polish Cabbage Soup

Sonia Hawkins
Amarillo, TX

A wonderful yummy recipe for a cool autumn day! You can change the flavor of the soup by using different types of sausage such as sage, andouille and so forth.

1 lb. hot or mild ground pork
    breakfast sausage
1 T. butter
10-3/4 oz. can tomato soup
10-1/2 oz. can beef broth
2-1/2 c. water
4 c. cabbage, shredded
1/2 c. onion, chopped

1/2 t. paprika
2 t. salt
1/8 t. pepper
1 bay leaf
Optional: 1 T. cooking sherry
Garnish: sour cream, saltine
    crackers

In a large soup pot over medium heat, brown sausage in butter. Add all ingredients except garnish. Stir gently, making sure cabbage is covered with liquid. Bring to a boil; reduce heat to low. Simmer for 30 to 45 minutes, stirring occasionally, until cabbage is as tender as desired. Discard bay leaf. Serve soup topped with a dollop of sour cream and crackers on the side. Makes 8 servings.

It's wonderful to have soup tucked away for a chilly day... why not make a double batch to freeze? Ladle cooled soup into plastic zipping bags, seal and press flat. When frozen, they'll stack easily, taking up little room in the freezer.

Corn, Sausage & Potato Chowder

Linda Belon
Wintersville, OH

Why go for fast food when you can put this chowder together so easily? Everyone loves it. We think it's best reheated a couple days later, so why not make it ahead of time to serve on an upcoming busy day? Yum!

1/2 lb. ground pork sausage
1 onion, finely chopped
3 potatoes, peeled and cubed
2 c. water
1/2 t. pepper

1/2 t. Italian seasoning
14-1/2 oz. can cream-style corn
15-1/2 oz. can corn, drained
12-oz. can evaporated milk

In a large stockpot over medium heat, crumble sausage and brown with onion; drain. Add potatoes, water and seasonings. Bring to a boil; reduce heat to medium-low. Simmer, covered, for about 20 minutes, until potatoes are tender. Stir in both cans of corn and evaporated milk. Simmer until heated through. Makes 4 to 6 servings.

Take a short drive into the country and go stargazing on a frosty autumn night. Late October is an especially good time to see shooting stars, but any clear night will provide a world of wonder overhead.

Tasty Fall Cooking

Barbecue Hot Dogs

Carol Heffner
Lexington, KY

My mother-in-law gave me this yummy recipe over 30 years ago and I have made it every Halloween since then. When my kids were little, it was a great meal before trick-or-treating. It has become a family tradition that I will pass on to my children.

1 c. onion, chopped
1/3 c. brown sugar, packed
1 T. vinegar
14-oz. bottle ketchup
16-oz. pkg. hot dogs
Optional: hot dog buns, split

In a lightly greased 13"x9" baking pan, combine all ingredients except hot dogs and buns. Mix well and add hot dogs. Bake, uncovered, at 300 degrees for one hour. May also combine ingredients in a 4-quart slow cooker; cover and cook on low setting for 4 to 6 hours. Serve on buns, if desired. Makes 8 servings.

Easy Hot Dog Sauce

Linda Wilcoxon
Nokesville, VA

I have been making this tangy sweet sauce for over 30 years! It only takes three ingredients, but it sends a grilled hot dog over the top. I make it for our Sunday School picnic bonfire held in the fall and it's always a hit.

1 lb. lean ground beef
1-1/4 to 1-1/2 c. catsup
3/4 c. brown sugar, packed, or to taste

Brown beef in a skillet over medium heat; drain. Add catsup and brown sugar to desired sweetness. Cook and stir until mixture simmers. Simmer about 10 minutes, stirring occasionally, until hot and flavors are well blended. Makes 12 servings.

Paint names on colorful mini gourds for whimsical placecards.

Soup Suppers

Oven-Baked Chili Dogs

Marsha Baker
Pioneer, OH

*These are a real hit with kids and adults alike! A friend
shared this wonderful recipe and we just love it. It's so
easy to make as few or as many as you'd like.*

8 whole-wheat hot dog buns,
   split
mayonnaise to taste
Optional: mustard, sweet pickle
   relish to taste

8 hot dogs
2 15-oz. cans favorite chili
2 c. shredded Cheddar cheese
1/2 onion, finely chopped

Spread the inside of each hot dog bun with mayonnaise. Add a stripe
of mustard and a dollop of relish, if desired. Fill buns with hot dogs.
Arrange in an aluminum foil-lined 13"x9" baking pan. Top hot dogs
evenly with chili, cheese and onion. Cover with more foil. Bake at
350 degrees for 45 minutes. Makes 8 servings.

For small-town games, there isn't always a lot of room for
a big tailgating party, so have a cookout beforehand! Everyone
can get in the spirit, enjoy some tasty food and then
walk to the game together.

Tasty Taco Soup

Sheri Kohl
Wentzville, MO

My family knows there's a nip of fall in the air when they come home and smell this hearty taco soup. It takes just minutes to toss in the slow cooker before work. We like it with mini cornbread muffins. It's also perfect to pack in a thermos for fall tailgates and picnics.

1 lb. ground beef
16-oz. can kidney beans
16-oz. can black beans
16-oz. can black-eyed peas or
   purple hull beans
16-oz. can mild chili beans
11-oz. can sweet corn with diced
   peppers
3 to 4 14-oz. cans chicken
   broth, divided
2 1-1/4 oz. pkgs. taco
   seasoning mix, divided
Garnish: shredded Cheddar
   cheese, sour cream

Brown beef in a large soup pot over medium heat; drain. Add all beans and corn; do not drain any of the cans. Stir in 2 cans chicken broth and one package taco seasoning. Bring to a boil over medium heat; reduce heat to medium-low. Simmer until heated through, about 30 minutes, stirring often. May also combine ingredients in a 6-quart slow cooker. Cover and cook on low setting for 8 hours. One hour before serving, stir in more broth if beans have soaked up too much liquid. May also stir in some or all of remaining taco seasoning to taste. Serve topped with cheese and a dollop of sour cream. Makes 8 servings.

Crunchy tortilla strips are a tasty addition to southwestern-style soups. Cut corn tortillas into thin strips, then deep-fry quickly. Drain on paper towels before sprinkling over bowls of soup. Try red or blue tortilla chips too!

Soup Suppers

Mexican Vegetable Soup

Vickie

Looking for a something a little different from chili? Try this!

1 lb. ground beef	16-oz. pkg frozen mixed
1-1/4 oz. pkg. taco seasoning	vegetables
mix	15 oz. can chili with hot beans
46-oz. can tomato juice	Garnish: shredded Cheddar
12-oz. can tomato paste	cheese, crushed corn chips

In a Dutch oven, brown beef over medium heat; drain. Add remaining ingredients except garnish; bring just to a boil. Reduce heat to low. Simmer for 20 to 25 minutes, until vegetables are tender, stirring occasionally. Top each serving with cheese and corn chips. Makes 10 servings.

Almost-Like-Cake Cornbread

Cindy Neel
Gooseberry Patch

I discovered this really moist mile-high cornbread recipe years ago, when we had an elderly neighbor who loved cornbread.

2 eggs, beaten	1-1/3 c. all-purpose flour
1/2 c. sugar	3/4 t. salt
1/2 c. butter, melted and slightly	1 c. buttermilk
cooled	4 t. baking powder
1-1/3 c. cornmeal	1 t. baking soda

In a large bowl, stir together eggs, sugar and melted butter. Alternately add cornmeal, flour and salt. Stir in buttermilk, baking powder and baking soda. Pour batter into a greased 8"x8" baking pan. Bake at 375 degrees for 25 to 30 minutes. Makes 12 to 16 servings.

Cornmeal comes in yellow, white and even blue...the choice is yours! Stone-ground cornmeal is more nutritious than regular cornmeal, but has a shorter shelf life.

Chicken & White Bean Soup

Emily Martin
Ontario, Canada

*This rich-tasting soup takes a little time, but it's well
worth it on a chilly autumn day.*

3 to 4-lb. stewing chicken
1 carrot, peeled and quartered
1 onion, quartered
1 stalk celery, quartered
12 to 14 c. water
2 to 3 15-1/2 oz. cans cannellini
    beans, drained and rinsed

1 c. onion, coarsely chopped
1 c. celery, sliced
1 clove garlic, minced
1/2 t. dried oregano
1 bay leaf
salt and pepper to taste

Place chicken in a large stockpot. Add carrot, quartered onion and
quartered celery stalk and enough water to cover. Bring to a boil over
high heat. Reduce heat to low; simmer for at least 2 hours, until
chicken is very tender. Remove chicken to a bowl to cool. Reserve
broth in stockpot. Strain, discarding vegetables. Remove chicken from
bones; chop and return to broth. Skim off any fat on top of broth. Stir
in remaining ingredients. Bring to a boil over high heat; reduce heat
to low. Simmer for 30 to 40 minutes. Just before serving, discard bay
leaf. Serves 10.

Polka-dot pumpkins! Hollow out pumpkins of two or three
different colors like orange, white and green. Punch out round
plugs from each pumpkin with an apple corer and just swap
the plugs between pumpkins.

Split Pea & Ham Soup

Shirley Howie
Foxboro, MA

This is a tummy-warming slow-cooker soup that I like to serve with crusty buttered bread. My husband requests this often!

2 c. cooked ham, cubed
1 c. dried split peas
1 c. onion, chopped
1 c. celery with leaves, chopped
1 c. carrot, peeled and shredded

1/2 t. dried thyme
1/4 t. pepper
1 bay leaf
4 c. chicken broth
2 c. water

Combine ham, dried peas, vegetables and seasonings in a 4-quart slow cooker. Pour chicken broth and water over all; stir. Cover and cook on low setting for 10 to 12 hours, or on high setting for 4 to 5 hours. Discard bay leaf before serving. Makes 6 servings.

Halloween was always such a fun time in the mountains of North Carolina. The air was crisp, the leaves were an abundant rainbow of color, pumpkins were everywhere and there were apples too. My mom always had us create our own costumes, so there was no telling what we would end up looking like! She always made candied or caramel apples for our cousins and the neighborhood kids, and we always looked forward to this treat. Halloween night would start out with soup and cornbread, and then the festivities would begin. House to house we would go until we were frozen, and then back home to warm up with hot chocolate and check out our bag of goodies. To this day, fall is still my favorite time of year...I still make caramel apples and fill my porch with pumpkins.

–Sophia Collins, Okeechobee, FL

Day-After-Thanksgiving Stew

Jennie Gist
Gooseberry Patch

*I've made this for several years with leftover holiday turkey
and we really enjoy it. Serve with hot buttered dinner rolls.*

3 T. butter
2 stalks celery, sliced
1 onion, diced
1 green pepper, diced
1 t. fresh thyme, chopped
1/4 t. salt
1/4 t. pepper

3 T. all-purpose flour
3 c. turkey or chicken broth
10-oz. pkg. frozen corn, thawed
10-oz. pkg. frozen baby lima
  beans, thawed
2 c. cooked turkey, diced
salt and pepper to taste

Melt butter in a stockpot over medium heat; add celery, onion and
green pepper. Sauté for 6 to 8 minutes, until softened and lightly
golden. Stir in thyme, salt and pepper. Sprinkle with flour; cook and
stir for 2 minutes. Stir in broth and simmer until slightly thickened,
10 to 15 minutes. Stir in corn, beans and turkey. Season again with
salt and pepper, as needed. Simmer about 30 minutes. Makes 6 to
8 servings.

Is there lots of leftover turkey? It freezes well for up to
3 months. Cut turkey into bite-size pieces, place in plastic
freezer bags and pop in the freezer...ready to stir into
hearty casseroles and soups whenever you are.

Soup Suppers

Cranberry Bread

Theda Light
Christiansburg, VA

I first found this recipe years ago in a storybook I was reading to my children. After reading it to my granddaughter one day, I decided to try the recipe. We loved it and it's now a must every year on our Thanksgiving table.

2 c. all-purpose flour
1 c. sugar
1-1/2 t. baking powder
1/2 t. baking soda
1 t. salt
1/4 c. butter

1 egg, beaten
1 t. orange zest
3/4 c. orange juice
3 c. fresh or frozen cranberries, chopped

Sift flour, sugar, baking powder, baking soda and salt into a large bowl. Cut in butter with a pastry cutter or a fork until mixture is crumbly. Add egg, orange zest and orange juice all at once; stir just until batter is evenly moistened. Fold in cranberries. Spoon batter into a greased 9"x5" loaf pan. Bake at 350 degrees for one hour and 10 minutes, or until a toothpick inserted in center comes out clean. Turn loaf out of pan; cool on a wire rack. Makes one loaf.

If you love fresh cranberries, stock up when they're available and pop unopened bags in the freezer. You'll be able to add their fruity tang to recipes year 'round.

Bratwurst Pretzel Reubens

Sarah Oravecz
Gooseberry Patch

We love these sandwiches...fun for an Oktoberfest cookout!
Sometimes I'll use my own home-baked soft pretzels, but I've found
soft pretzels from the grocery's freezer section are good too.

4 bratwursts, halved lengthwise
4 large soft pretzels, warmed if
   frozen
spicy brown mustard to taste
4 T. butter, divided

4 T. olive oil, divided
8 to 16 slices Muenster cheese
1 c. sauerkraut, well drained
pepper to taste

Grill or pan-fry bratwursts as desired; set aside. Meanwhile, slice
pretzels in half horizontally; spread the cut sides with mustard. Working
in batches, melt one tablespoon butter with one tablespoon olive oil in
a skillet over medium-low heat. Add 2 pretzel halves to skillet, crust-
side down. Arrange one to 2 cheese slices on each half. Cook just until
cheese is nearly melted. With a spatula, remove pretzel halves to a
plate. Top one pretzel half with a bratwurst; spoon on 1/4 cup
sauerkraut. Season with pepper. Add pretzel top. Repeat with
remaining ingredients. Makes 4 servings.

Skip the disposable party plates...set out a stack of vintage
tin pie plates instead! They won't turn soggy with juicy
sandwiches and can be used again & again.

Soup Suppers

Sweet & Gold Potato Chowder

Deborah Mahon
Delaware, OH

Homemade potato soup was a common meal on the farm in Ohio where I grew up, and where I learned to cook with my grandmother and mother. I've added sweet potatoes, Yukon golds and a sprinkle of bacon to make it special.

5 slices bacon, chopped
4 cloves garlic. minced
1 onion, chopped
3 14-1/2 oz. cans chicken broth
4 sweet potatoes, peeled and
   chopped
4 Yukon Gold potatoes, chopped
2 stalks celery, chopped

2 carrots, peeled and chopped
salt and pepper to taste
2 c. half-and-half
3 T. butter, sliced
1 T. cornstarch
1/4 c. cold water
Optional: red pepper flakes

In a large stockpot over medium-high heat, cook bacon until crisp; remove bacon to a paper towel with a slotted spoon. Reserve 3 to 4 tablespoons drippings in skillet. Reduce heat to medium. Add garlic and onion; cook for 2 to 3 minutes, until tender. Add chicken broth, add all potatoes, celery and carrots. Simmer until vegetables are tender, 25 to 30 minutes. Season with salt and pepper. Stir in half-and half and butter. In a small bowl, whisk cornstarch into cold water; gently stir into chowder and cook until thickened. Add crumbled bacon, reserving some for garnish. Simmer over low heat for an additional 5 to 7 minutes, stirring often. Sprinkle portions with reserved bacon and red pepper flakes, if desired. Makes 6 to 8 servings.

For a fruity cream cheese spread, combine one 8-ounce package of softened cream cheese with 1/4 cup apricot preserves. Stir until smooth. So delicious on warm slices of quick bread!

Speedy Bouillabaisse

Peggy Lopes
Cranston, RI

This simple recipe is special to me because it is served every Thanksgiving Day, when all our family is together. It takes just 30 minutes or less.

10-3/4 oz. can cream of celery soup
10-3/4 oz. can cream of chicken soup
2 c. light cream
6-oz. pkg. frozen king crabmeat, thawed and drained

5-oz. can tiny shrimp, drained
7-3/4 oz. can oysters, drained and 1/4 c. liquid reserved
1 t. onion salt
1/4 t. seasoned pepper

Combine soups and cream in a double boiler over hot water. Cook and stir until blended. Stir in crabmeat, shrimp, oysters with reserved liquid and seasonings. Heat through. Serves 6.

Children's Bag Bread

Jenelle Witmer
Richland, PA

When my children get restless I mix this up and let them play. They love to squish the bag, they've even stomped on it or played pitch and catch with it. They love playing with gooey stuff!

1 env. active dry yeast
1 c. very warm water, 110 to 115 degrees
2 T. honey

2 T. oil
2-1/2 c. all-purpose flour
1 t. salt

In a cup, combine yeast, warm water, honey and oil. Stir well; let stand for 5 minutes. Combine flour and salt in a one-gallon plastic zipping bag; shake to mix. Add yeast mixture to bag. Press air out of bag; seal and squeeze bag until well kneaded. Let dough rise in bag for 30 to 45 minutes, Shape dough into a loaf; place in a greased 9"x5" loaf pan. Let rise again until double. Bake at 350 degrees for 30 minutes, or until golden. Makes one loaf.

Soup Suppers

Quick Clam Chowder

Lisa Cunningham
Boothbay, ME

This quick soup really warms you up on a cool day. It's a broth-based chowder, as we like it here in Maine. If you like a creamy chowder, add a cup of half-and-half in the last five minutes and heat through. It's good either way.

4 6-1/2 oz. cans chopped clams, drained and juice reserved
8-oz. bottle clam juice
4 Yukon Gold potatoes, peeled and diced
1 onion, diced

1 T. butter
1 T. olive oil
2 T. fresh parsley, chopped
Optional: saltine or oyster crackers

Add reserved and bottled clam juice to a large saucepan over medium heat. Add potatoes; bring to a boil. Reduce heat to low; simmer until potatoes are fork-tender. Meanwhile, in a small skillet over medium heat, cook onion with butter and oil until soft and lightly golden. Add onion mixture and clams to potato mixture. Simmer for 15 minutes. Stir in parsley; simmer another 5 minutes. Serve with crackers. Makes 4 servings.

Savory herbed crackers make any bowl of soup even more delicious. Toss together 1-1/2 cups oyster crackers, 1-1/2 tablespoons melted butter, 1/4 teaspoon dried thyme and 1/4 teaspoon garlic powder. Spread on a baking sheet and bake at 350 degrees for about 10 minutes, until crunchy and golden.

Pot Roast Soup

Andrea Heyart
Savannah, TX

Coming home to a simmering slow cooker of soup on a chilly night is one of life's great pleasures. Much like actual pot roast, this hearty soup almost tastes better the next day! Serve with crusty bread or dinner rolls.

2 lbs. lean stew beef cubes
1 white or yellow onion, diced
1 T. butter
2 10-oz. cans diced tomatoes
　　with green chiles
2 c. frozen diced potatoes, plain
　　or with onions and green
　　peppers
4 c. beef broth

1 T. garlic, minced
1/2 t. dried thyme
1/4 t. dried basil
1/4 t. salt, or more to taste
1/8 t. pepper
3/4 c. frozen sliced or diced
　　carrots
1/4 t. Worcestershire sauce

In a large skillet over medium heat, sauté beef and onion in butter until beef is lightly browned and onion is translucent. Transfer beef mixture to a 6-quart slow cooker; add remaining ingredients. Cover and cook on low setting for 8 hours. Season with more salt and pepper, if needed. Makes 6 servings.

If frost is in the forecast, you can still save the herbs in the garden! Spoon chopped fresh herbs into an ice cube tray, one tablespoon per cube. Cover with water and freeze. Frozen cubes can be added directly to hot soups or stews for a pop of fresh flavor.

Fall
Soup Suppers

Easy Cloverleaf Yeast Rolls

Linda Rich
Bean Station, TN

I cook Sunday lunch for my family of 14 almost every Sunday. They are spoiled by these rolls! So when I found this recipe in a local church cookbook, I felt like I had hit the jackpot. I make the dough on Saturday night before bedtime and prepare the rolls before church on Sunday morning. By the time I return from services three hours later, the rolls are ready to bake. The dough can be adapted to make cinnamon rolls also.

6 c. bread flour
1 c. sugar
1 T. salt
3 envs. active dry yeast

1/2 c. shortening
2-1/2 c. very warm water,
    110 to 115 degrees, divided
Garnish: melted butter

In a very large bowl, mix together flour, sugar, salt and yeast. Cut in shortening with a pastry blender until well mixed. Add 2 cups very warm water; mix with a wooden spoon. Add remaining water as needed to make dough soft and workable. Cover bowl and refrigerate for 6 hours to overnight. About 3 to 4 hours before serving time, brush muffin tins with melted butter. Pour out dough onto a floured surface. Shape into marble-size balls; place 3 balls in each muffin cup. Drizzle additional melted butter over each roll. Cover with a tea towel; allow to rise 3 hours in a warm area. Bake at 325 degrees for 20 to 25 minutes. May bake only part of dough; refrigerate remaining dough for 3 to 5 days. Makes 4 dozen.

Cinnamon Rolls:

Roll out desired amount of dough on a floured surface. Brush with melted butter; sprinkle with brown sugar, cinnamon, nuts and/or raisins. Roll up dough and slice. Place slices in a buttered baking pan or muffin cups. Allow to rise and bake as above.

Baking yeast bread from scratch? A convenient place to let the dough rise is inside your microwave. Heat a mug of water on high for 2 minutes. Then remove the mug, place the covered bowl of dough inside and close the door.

White Turkey & Bean Chili

Tara Johnson
Logan, UT

My family loves white chicken chili, but one day I didn't have chicken breast on hand so I used some ground turkey. It made a meatier-tasting chili. I've made it for parties at work and everyone wants the recipe! Sometimes I'll add my homemade tomato salsa, instead of the green salsa. Add whatever vegetables you like, I've added zucchini and celery...have fun with it!

4 c. chicken broth
4 to 6 15.8-oz. cans Great
    Northern beans
2 4-oz. cans chopped green
    chiles
1 bunch fresh cilantro, chopped
1 lb. ground turkey

2 onions, chopped
2 green peppers, chopped
2 c. salsa verde
1-oz. pkg, turkey gravy mix
1/2 t. chili powder
1/2 t. seasoned salt
1/2 t. garlic pepper

Add chicken broth, beans, green chiles and cilantro to a 6-quart slow cooker; turn to high setting. In a skillet over medium heat, brown turkey, onions and green peppers. Drain; stir in remaining ingredients and add to slow cooker. Cover and cook on high setting for 4 to 6 hours, until soup starts to boil. Makes 12 to 16 servings.

For a quick fall centerpiece, set a spicy-scented orange pillar candle in a shallow dish. Surround with hazelnuts or acorns...done!

Soup Suppers

Hawaiian BBQ Beef

Rebecca Gonzalez
Moreno Valley, CA

My mom used to make this for special occasions like football parties and such! A slow cooker makes it a snap. If you don't have a really large slow cooker, the brisket and other ingredients could be halved between two 4 or 5-quart smaller slow cookers, same cooktime.

6 to 8-lb. beef brisket
20-oz. bottle Hawaiian
   barbecue sauce

16-oz. jar salsa
1.35-oz. pkg. onion soup mix
hoagie rolls, split

Spray an 8-quart slow cooker with non-stick vegetable spray; add brisket. Combine remaining ingredients in a bowl; mix well and spoon over brisket. Cover and cook on low setting for 6 to 8 hours, until brisket falls apart. Shred brisket; serve on hoagie rolls. Makes 20 to 25 sandwiches.

Chicken Pepperoncini

Sue Neely
Greenville, IL

This is a great-tasting slow-cooker recipe! My family just loves it and it can be served different ways...nice any time of year. You can even serve the shredded chicken on a bed of lettuce.

2-1/2 to 3 lbs. chicken tenders
   or boneless, skinless chicken
   breasts
1 to 2 16-oz. jars pepperoncini
   peppers

0.7-oz. pkg. Italian salad
   dressing mix
split sandwich buns or
   flour tortillas

Place chicken in a 5-quart slow cooker; top with desired amount of pepperoncini with juice, depending on spiciness desired. Sprinkle with dressing mix. Cover and cook on low setting for 6 to 8 hours. Just before serving, shred chicken with peppers, or discard peppers, if preferred. To serve, spoon chicken mixture onto buns or into tortillas. Makes 4 to 6 servings.

3-Day Vegetable Stew

Brenda Wells
Summerville, SC

Summer finds us with a lot of fresh veggies on hand! Between my own garden and neighbors who would leave bags of veggies on the porch, we needed to find different ways to use them while they were fresh. I decided a stew would keep us happy. We make this on Sunday evenings so my husband can take some to work. Especially good in cold weather.

2 32-oz. containers beef broth
2 onions, diced
3 potatoes, peeled and cut into
    1-inch cubes
1 lb. baby carrots, sliced
2 11-oz. cans corn, drained
16-oz. can green beans, drained
15-1/2 oz. can petite diced
    tomatoes
1 T. garlic powder
1/2 t. dried thyme

1/2 t. salt
1/2 t. pepper
2 zucchini, halved lengthwise
    and thinly sliced
1 yellow squash, halved
    lengthwise and thinly sliced
3 to 4 stalks celery, chopped
1 green pepper, diced
1/2 head cabbage, shredded
1 T. cornstarch
1/4 c. cold water

In a stockpot, combine beef broth, onions, potatoes, carrots, corn, green beans, tomatoes with juice and seasonings. Bring to a boil over high heat. Reduce heat to low; cover with a vented lid. Simmer for about 30 minutes, skimming any foam that may rise to the top. Add zucchini, squash, celery and green pepper; simmer for 15 minutes. Add cabbage; cook about 10 minutes. For a thicker soup, dissolve cornstarch in cold water; add to stew and cook until thickened. Tastes best the next day and keeps well in refrigerator; reheat only the amount desired. Makes 16 servings.

Ask Thanksgiving guests to bring canned goods to dinner. Delivered to a shelter, they're a wonderful way to begin the holiday season.

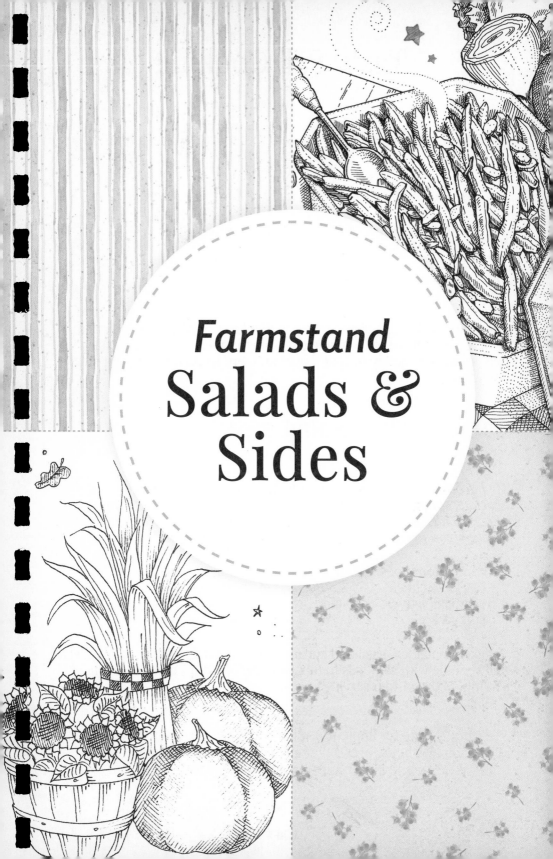

Farmstand
Salads &
Sides

End-of-Summer Slaw

Nancy Christensen
Mission, TX

Crisp, sweet-tart apples add a taste of fall to a potluck favorite.

4 c. shredded coleslaw mix
2 Granny Smith apples, cored
   and cubed
1/4 c. green onions, sliced
3 T. sugar

3 T. cider vinegar
2 T. oil
1/4 t. apple pie spice
1/4 t. salt

Combine coleslaw, apples and onions in a large bowl; toss to mix and set aside. For dressing, combine remaining ingredients. Pour dressing over salad; toss gently to coat. Cover and refrigerate until serving time. Serves 10.

Tasty Tomato Salad

Marianne DiNardo
Putnam Valley, NY

My husband's Italian family taught me how to make this simple, delicious salad when we were newlyweds. I've shared it with many of my friends and they all love it! It is especially tasty to dip some crusty bread in the leftover olive oil at the bottom of the bowl.

2 to 3 ripe tomatoes, cut into
   bite-size cubes
4 fresh basil leaves, or to taste,
   snipped

1 cucumber, peeled and sliced
1/4 c. olive oil
salt to taste

Combine tomatoes, basil and cucumber in a bowl. Drizzle with olive oil and sprinkle with salt; toss to mix well. Let stand 30 minutes before serving. Makes 4 to 6 servings.

Autumn is time for apple fun. Pick your own apples in an orchard, watch cider being pressed at a cider mill or go to a small-town apple butter stirring. Don't forget to taste!

Salads & Sides

Cornbread Salad

Sandra Turner
Fayetteville, NC

This is my go-to dish for our church potlucks...I always bring home an empty bowl. It's a layered salad that is pretty served in a large clear bowl. I love that I can make this the day before the event.

8-1/2 oz. pkg. corn muffin mix
2 15-oz. cans pinto beans,
   drained
2 15-oz. cans corn, drained
3 ripe tomatoes, chopped
   and divided
1/2 c. green onions, chopped
   and divided

2.8-oz. pkg. real bacon bits,
   divided
8-oz. pkg. shredded Cheddar
   cheese, divided
16-oz. bottle ranch salad
   dressing, divided

Prepare and bake corn muffin mix according to package directions, using an 8"x8" baking pan; cool. Crumble half the cornbread into a large bowl. Top with one can beans, one can corn, half the tomatoes, half the onions, half the bacon and half the cheese. Top with half the ranch dressing; spread smoothly. Repeat layers. Cover and chill for 2 hours to overnight before serving. Makes 12 to 15 servings.

Head to the great outdoors for a family potluck! Toss lots of colorful blankets and quilts on the tables and then after lunch, play games or take a nature hike while the leaves are at their prettiest.

Buffet Relish Salad

Joan Chance
Houston, TX

This recipe comes from my mom. I'm 81 and when I was young, I actually did not care for this. But as an adult I enjoy it! Other vegetables may be used, such as red peppers instead of green.

15-oz. can small petite peas
15-oz. can white shoepeg corn
14-oz. can bean sprouts
8-oz. can sliced water chestnuts
7-oz. can sliced mushrooms

1 green pepper, chopped
1 onion, chopped
1 c. carrots, peeled and sliced
1 c. celery, sliced
3/4 c. cauliflower, sliced

Drain all canned vegetables; combine in a large bowl. Add remaining ingredients. Pour Marinade over all; toss well to mix. Cover and refrigerate for 24 hours before serving. Stir again just before serving. Makes 10 to 12 servings.

Marinade:

2-1/2 c. white vinegar
1 c. oil
2 c. sugar

4 t. salt
1/8 t. pepper

Combine all ingredients in a saucepan over medium heat. Cook to just boiling, stirring until sugar dissolves.

Look for apple cider vinegar at autumn farmstands. It's useful in so many ways like pickling and making salad dressing. Add a splash to cooked vegetables or a dash to skillet drippings when making gravy.

Mary's Romaine & Bacon Salad

Diana Krol
Nickerson, KS

This salad is especially good with roast chicken and pork.

2 heads romaine lettuce, torn
1/2 lb. bacon, crisply cooked and
    crumbled
2 11-oz. can mandarin oranges,
    drained

4-oz. container crumbled
    blue cheese
3/4 c. chopped walnuts
2 green onions, chopped

In a large bowl, combine all ingredients. Pour Red Wine Dressing over all; toss gently before serving. Serves 8.

Red Wine Dressing:

1 c. sugar
1 c. oil
1/2 c. red wine vinegar

1/2 t. salt
1/8 t. paprika

Combine all ingredients in a blender; process well.

Don't let day-old bread go to waste! Cut it into cubes, pack into freezer bags and freeze. It's perfect for making herbed salad croutons, a savory stuffing or even bread pudding.

Aunt Connie's Greek Salad

Jan Sherwood
Carpentersville, IL

Aunt Connie was a favorite in our family. Whenever I make this recipe that she shared, I remember sitting at her picnic table, enjoying good food and even better conversation. This is a great make-ahead dish.

7-oz. jar broken stuffed salad
   olives, well drained
6-oz. can black olives, sliced
   and drained
1 c. celery, chopped
1 c. green pepper, chopped

1 c. onion, chopped
2/3 c. olive oil
1/3 c. red wine vinegar
2 cloves garlic, minced
dried oregano, cayenne pepper,
   salt and pepper to taste

Combine all ingredients in a large bowl; mix well. Cover and and refrigerate. Best made 24 hours in advance to allow flavors to blend. Serves 10.

Our son and his wife live on a farm. Garry & Brianne have added many nice touches to their home, including a lovely water garden in the field at the front of the house. The frogs love this lush and tranquil little pond and every summer, many frogs make it their home. Unfortunately, the pond isn't deep enough for them to successfully hibernate, so every fall, Brianne and I gather up all the frogs and relocate them to a nearby creek that runs into the channel. The creek is frog heaven and deep enough that they can survive our long cold winters. The first year we did this, I didn't know that Brianne was afraid of frogs:...she never let on and just kept on trying to catch them. Now we are both pros at rescuing the frogs and look forward every year to our "frog rescue day." It feels good to do our part in maintaining the wetlands in our environment and we have so much fun doing it. The frogs don't seem to mind it either!

–Janis Parr, Ontario, Canada

Salads & Sides

Frozen Cucumber Salad

Teri Lindquist
Gurnee, IL

I have been making this delicious salad for over 20 years, ever since we had a vegetable garden. We'd grow these ingredients just to be able to have this salad close at hand all year long. I love to open my freezer door and see containers of this wonderful salad.

8 c. cucumbers, thinly sliced and
    divided
1 T. salt, divided
1 onion, thinly sliced
1 c. green pepper, thinly sliced

1 c. celery, thinly sliced
2 c. sugar
1 c. white vinegar
1 T. mustard seed
2 t. celery seed

In a large colander, layer cucumber slices, sprinkling about 1/2 teaspoon salt on each layer. Let stand in the sink for 30 to 60 minutes to drain. Rinse lightly; gently press out any remaining liquid. In a large bowl, toss cucumbers with onion, green pepper and celery; set aside. In a separate bowl, whisk together remaining ingredients until sugar is dissolved. Pour over cucumber mixture and stir gently. Divide cucumbers among 1/2-pint or one-pint plastic freezer containers; spoon marinade evenly over each. Seal tightly; freeze for up to 6 months. To serve, thaw a container in the refrigerator overnight. Makes 3 to 4 quarts.

Create a fall centerpiece in a snap! Hot-glue ears of
mini Indian corn around a terra-cotta pot and set a vase
of orange or yellow mums in the center.

Mom's Fiesta Corn Salad

Ramona Wysong
Barlow, KY

This is a recipe from my mom and my grandmother. It's great for something a little different with corn...nice for family get-togethers and celebrations.

15-oz. can white shoepeg corn, drained
15-oz. can yellow corn, drained
2-oz. jar diced pimentos, drained

1 c. onion, chopped
1 c. green pepper, chopped
3/4 c. sweet pickles, chopped

Combine all vegetables in a large bowl. Pour Marinade/Salad Dressing over vegetables; toss well to mix. Cover and refrigerate until serving time. Serves 8.

Marinade/Salad Dressing:

1 c. oil
1 c. white vinegar
1/2 c. water
1 c. sugar
1 t. dried parsley

1 t. seasoning salt
1 t. salt
1/4 t. white pepper
1 t. black pepper
1 t. celery seed

Combine all ingredients in a saucepan over medium heat. Cook and stir until sugar dissolves; bring to a boil for one minute. Cool to lukewarm before using.

Packing for a picnic or a tailgating party? Safety first!
Keep hot foods hot, cold foods cold, and don't let any food
sit out longer than 2 hours, even if the food looks just fine.

Salads & Sides

Mexican Slaw

Deb Sparks
Cleveland, OK

This is a great recipe to enjoy with Mexican dinners, hamburgers, sandwiches and other casual meals. We love it! The first time I tasted this slaw was on Thanksgiving a few years ago. We all felt it was an odd choice for our holiday dinner, but we fell in love with it. Any time I take it to a church dinner, I always have at least one request for this very easy recipe.

14-oz. pkg. shredded coleslaw
    mix
11-oz. can sweet corn & diced
    peppers, drained
1/2 to 3/4 c. red onion, chopped
8-oz. pkg. shredded mild
    Cheddar cheese

1 bunch fresh cilantro, chopped,
    or to taste
3-oz. pkg. ramen noodles,
    uncooked

In a large bowl, combine coleslaw, corn, onion and cheese. Add desired amount of cilantro; toss to mix and set aside. Crush ramen noodles, discarding ramen seasoning packet. Stir in uncooked noodles just before pouring Lime Ranch Dressing over slaw. Pour dressing over slaw; mix well. Serves 10 to 12.

Lime Ranch Dressing:

8-oz. bottle ranch salad
    dressing

2 T. lime juice
1 to 2 t. ground cumin

Mix together all ingredients.

The simplest table decorations are often the most charming! Fill a rustic wooden bowl with shiny red apples for the kitchen table, or pile the bowl with bright-colored balls of yarn for a crafting corner.

Avocado-Pineapple Salad

Jill Ball
Highland, UT

This is the easiest and yummiest recipe. It looks fancy,
but is a breeze to make!

8 c. arugula or romaine lettuce,
    torn, or spring mix
3 c. pineapple, peeled and diced
2 avocados, halved and diced
1/2 c. green onions, chopped

1 T. lemon juice
1 T. olive oil
ground cumin, salt and pepper
    to taste
Garnish: chopped fresh mint

In a large bowl, combine lettuce, pineapple, avocados and onions; set
aside. Whisk together lemon juice, olive oil and seasonings in a small
bowl. Drizzle lemon juice mixture over salad; toss gently. Sprinkle with
mint. Makes 6 to 8 servings.

For the best of the bounty, head to the pumpkin patch early!
Just fill a wheelbarrow with pumpkins, squash and gourds for
an oh-so-simple harvest decoration. Add some fun with white
Lumina pumpkins or orange-red Cinderella pumpkins.

Salads & Sides

Gee Gee's Heavenly Hash

Ronda Hauss
Louisville, KY

My Grandma Cora always made this fruit salad for Thanksgiving and everyone loved it. She passed away many years ago. Recently my Uncle Ron found Grandma's small recipe box and gave it to me. Her Heavenly Hash recipe was inside! I'm so happy to add it to my holiday table!

2 15-oz. cans crushed pineapple
2 15-oz. cans fruit cocktail, drained and juice reserved
2 15-1/4 oz. cans sliced peaches, drained and juice reserved
2 8-1/4 oz. cans mandarin oranges, drained and juice reserved

3-oz. jar maraschino cherries, drained and juice reserved
8-oz. container sour cream
8-oz. container frozen whipped topping, thawed
10-oz. pkg. mini marshmallows

Add undrained pineapple to a large bowl; set aside. Add remaining drained fruit, sour cream and whipped topping; stir gently to mix. Cover and refrigerate overnight; combine and refrigerate reserved fruit juice. One hour before serving time, stir in marshmallows. Add some of the reserved fruit juice if a thinner consistency is desired. Serves 8 to 10.

For a centerpiece in a jiffy, round up any wide glass vases or hurricanes. Fill them with colorful gourds and pumpkins...done!

Reliable Pasta Salad

Patricia Nau
River Grove, IL

*Our neighborhood grocery & deli was really special. All of the food
and desserts were made from scratch by the ladies in the deli. When
the grocery closed 12 years ago, I asked the deli ladies if someone
would give me the recipe for their pasta salad. Voilà! My entire family
loves this salad. By the way, use all green peppers, if you wish...
we like the rainbow color of the different peppers!*

16-oz. pkg. linguine pasta,
   uncooked and broken in half
3 tomatoes, chopped
1 green pepper, chopped
1 yellow pepper, chopped
1 orange pepper, chopped
1 red pepper, chopped

2 seedless cucumbers, chopped
1 bunch green onions, chopped
16-oz. bottle Italian salad
   dressing
2.6-oz. jar salad seasoning
2 t. sugar

Cook pasta according to package directions; drain and rinse with cold
water. Transfer pasta to a large bowl; add remaining ingredients.
Mix well. Cover and refrigerate overnight. Mix again before serving.
Leftovers keep well in the refrigerator. Makes 8 to 10 servings.

To keep wooden salad bowls looking their best, rub them
inside and out with wax paper after washing them with warm,
soapy water. The wax from the paper will keep the surface
of the bowl sealed.

Salads & Sides

Sweet-and-Sour Macaroni Salad

Lynn Foley
Branson, MO

This is a great side for almost any meat and so easy to make!
It feeds a crowd and keeps really well in the fridge.

8-oz. pkg. elbow macaroni,
   uncooked
1 c. water
1/4 c. cider vinegar
1 c. sugar

1/2 c. Italian salad dressing
1 cucumber, coarsely chopped
1 tomato, coarsely chopped
1 onion, coarsely chopped

Cook macaroni according to package directions; drain and rinse with cold water. Meanwhile, in a saucepan over medium heat, bring water, vinegar and sugar to a boil, mixing well. Remove pan from heat; add salad dressing. Set aside and cool completely. Combine vegetables in a large bowl; add macaroni and dressing mixture. Toss well. Cover and refrigerate for several hours to overnight. Serves 12 to 16.

Choose a crisp fall evening to host a bonfire party for friends of all ages. Serve baked beans and hot cider, roast hot dogs, sing songs together and tell ghost stories...every hometown has a few! You'll be making memories that will last a lifetime.

Church Social Potato Salad

Janis Parr
Ontario, Canada

This is a very old country recipe for a tasty potato salad enjoyed at many church socials in these parts. There will be no leftovers! It's made one day ahead of serving, which is very convenient. Salad is nice when placed in a lettuce-lined bowl. Slices of hard-boiled egg placed in a ring on top of salad add a finishing touch.

6 potatoes, peeled and cut into thirds	1 egg, beaten
1/2 t. salt	1/2 c. onion, minced
1/2 c. white vinegar	2/3 c. milk
2/3 c. sugar	salt and pepper to taste

Add potatoes and salt to a large saucepan of boiling water. Cook over medium-high heat until fork-tender; drain. Meanwhile, in a small saucepan over medium heat, combine vinegar and sugar. Cook just until mixture starts to boil; remove from heat. While potatoes are still hot, mash well; add hot vinegar mixture and stir well. Add egg and stir to combine; the heat from the potatoes will cook the egg. Stir in onion and milk. Mixture will be loose. Season with salt and pepper. Allow to cool slightly; cover and chill until ready to serve. Makes 6 servings.

Tie up festive bundles of flatware for a potluck or picnic. Wrap silverware in a colorful cloth napkins and tie with jute. Place in a rustic tin pail or wicker basket at the end of the buffet line.

Salads & Sides

Corn & Black Bean Salad

Diane Skidmore
Visalia, CA

This is my dad's favorite salad for barbecues. So easy, so tasty and can be made the day before the party!

15-1/4 oz. can corn, drained
15-oz. can black beans, drained
   and rinsed
1 red pepper, chopped
1 tomato, chopped
6 green onions, chopped
1/2 c. red onion, chopped
Optional: 1 jalapeño pepper,
   seeded and finely chopped

1 clove garlic, minced
3/4 c. Italian salad dressing
1 T. fresh cilantro or parsley,
   minced
1 T. lime or lemon juice
3/4 t. hot pepper sauce
1/2 t. chili powder

Combine all vegetables in a large bowl; set aside. In a small bowl, combine remaining ingredients; pour over corn mixture and toss to coat. Cover and refrigerate at least 6 hours to overnight. Serve with a slotted spoon. Serves 6 to 8.

For hearty salads in a snap, keep unopened cans of diced tomatoes, black olives, garbanzo beans and marinated artichokes in the fridge. They'll be chilled and ready to toss with fresh greens at a moment's notice.

Tasty Fall Cooking

Bacon-Broccoli Salad

Michelle Powell
Valley, AL

A hearty salad that everyone will love. Men really go for it!

10 slices bacon, crisply cooked
   and crumbled
2 bunches broccoli, finely
   chopped
3 3-1/4 oz. cans sliced black
   olives, drained
1 bunch green onions, finely
   chopped

1 c. mayonnaise
1/4 c. mayonnaise-style salad
   dressing
3/4 c. shredded Parmesan
   cheese
Italian salad dressing to taste

Combine bacon and vegetables in a large bowl; set aside. In a separate
bowl, combine mayonnaise, mayonnaise-style salad dressing and
Parmesan cheese. Spoon over vegetables; stir until all ingredients are
moistened. Thin with Italian dressing as desired. Cover and refrigerate
overnight. Serves 12.

Zesty Cucumber Salad

Jill Ball
Highland, UT

This is a yummy easy salad. I admit it...I stand at the fridge,
fork in hand, and eat it straight from the container!

1 red onion, halved and
   thinly sliced
3 T. rice vinegar, divided
3 cucumbers, peeled and
   thinly sliced

1/4 t. salt
2 T. olive oil
2 T. fresh dill, chopped
salt and pepper to taste

In a small bowl, toss onion with one tablespoon vinegar; set aside.
Place cucumbers in a colander and toss with salt. Drain for 10 minutes;
pat dry. Combine onion and cucumbers in a large bowl. Toss with olive
oil and remaining vinegar. Add dill; season with salt and pepper. Cover
and chill until ready to serve. Makes 8 servings.

Salads & Sides

Sweet Coleslaw

Liz Plotnick-Snay
Gooseberry Patch

We love this light coleslaw! It's perfect for barbecues and picnics on hot sunny days, since it has no mayonnaise.

4 c. cabbage, shredded
1/4 c. green onion, sliced
1/2 c. green pepper, chopped
1/2 c. yellow pepper, chopped
1/2 c. red pepper, chopped
1/3 c. sugar
1/4 c. canola oil

1/4 c. vinegar
1 t. salt
3/4 t. dried dill weed
1/2 t. mustard seed
1/2 t. celery seed
1/4 to 1/3 c. roasted peanuts

Combine cabbage, onion and peppers in a large bowl; set aside. In a small bowl, combine remaining ingredients except peanuts; stir until well blended. Pour over vegetables and toss. Cover and chill. Add peanuts just before serving; toss lightly. Makes 6 servings.

Toting a salad to a get-together? Mix it up in a plastic zipping bag, seal and set it on ice in a picnic cooler. When you arrive, pour out the salad into a serving bowl. No worries about leaks or spills!

Rose's 3-Bean Dish

Diane Holland
Galena, IL

Everyone loves these beans and asks for the recipe. The recipe was given to me by my sister-in-law many years ago. Add a pound of browned hamburger to this if you like.

1/2 lb. bacon
1-1/2 c. onions, diced
1/2 c. brown sugar, packed
1 T. dry mustard
1/2 t. garlic powder
1/2 t. salt

2 16-oz. cans butter beans, drained
16-oz. can Boston baked beans, drained
14-1/2 oz. can lima beans, drained

In a large skillet over medium heat, cook bacon until crisp. Remove bacon to paper towels; partially drain skillet. Add onions to drippings in skillet; cook until lightly golden. Remove onions with a slotted spoon. Add brown sugar and seasonings to skillet; cook and stir until brown sugar dissolves. Return onions and crumbled bacon to skillet; add beans. Stir well and heat through over medium-low heat. Makes 10 servings.

A sweet placecard how-to...preserve dried leaves by ironing between 2 sheets of wax paper under a tea towel. When cool, trim around the leaves and write guests' names on with metallic ink.

Salads & Sides

Farmers' Market BBQ

Barbara Bargdill
Gooseberry Patch

We love to cook out in our backyard all fall, almost until the snow starts to fly! This makes a scrumptious change from potato sides. It's great for guests looking for a meatless main too...just spoon it over savory rice. Feel free to mix & match the veggies!

1 bunch broccoli, cut into
   bite-size flowerets
2 redskin potatoes, thinly sliced
1/2 lb. sliced mushrooms
2 carrots, peeled and thinly
   sliced
1 onion, thinly sliced

1 zucchini, thinly sliced
1 yellow squash, thinly sliced
1 green pepper, thinly sliced
1 red pepper, thinly sliced
1 to 2 T. olive oil, as needed
salt and pepper to taste

Combine all vegetables in a large grill-safe pan. Drizzle with olive oil. Season with salt and pepper; toss to coat. Cover and refrigerate about 2 hours. Grill, covered, over medium-high heat until vegetables are tender, about 6 to 10 minutes. May also transfer vegetables onto a piece of aluminum foil placed on grill. Cover grill and cook as above. Serves 6.

In the mood for a cookout, but it's too chilly outside? Use a stovetop grill pan indoors. Many recipes intended for a gas or charcoal grill can be prepared in a grill pan, so give it a try!

Fried Green Tomato Casserole
Donna Clement
Daphne, AL

This is a delicious twist on fried green tomatoes that you will want to fix again & again. A friend from the Mississippi Gulf Coast taught me how to make it.

1/4 t. Cajun seasoning
1/4 t. garlic powder
1/4 t. lemon pepper seasoning
1 t. kosher salt
1/4 t. pepper
4 green tomatoes, thickly sliced

1 c. sweet onion, chopped
2 c. shredded Cheddar cheese
1 sleeve round buttery crackers, crushed
1/4 c. butter, melted

Combine all seasonings in a cup; set aside. In a lightly greased 13"x9" baking pan, layer half the tomatoes, half of seasoning mixture, half the onion and half the cheese. Repeat layers. Top with crackers; drizzle with melted butter. Bake, covered, at 400 degrees for 45 minutes; uncover and bake for 15 more minutes. Makes 8 servings.

George's Shortcut Zucchini Gratin
Stephanie Dardani-D'Esposito
Ravena, NY

My dad used to make this for me when I was little...it was the only way I would eat zucchini! Now that I am a mom, I continue to make this quick and yummy dish for my family.

1 T. olive oil
2 to 3 zucchini, thinly sliced
1 t. onion powder

1/2 t. salt
1/4 t. pepper
1/2 c. grated Parmesan cheese

Heat oil in a saucepan over medium-high heat; add zucchini. Cover and cook for 7 to 10 minutes, until zucchini is softened. Add seasonings; sauté until zucchini is tender. Sprinkle with Parmesan cheese; let stand until melted. Serves 5.

Salads & Sides

Versatile Zucchini Patties

Kathy Farrell
Rochester, NY

This is a great way to get your kids to try zucchini! I have made this recipe so many times, I don't need to look at my recipe card anymore. We love it as a side dish. We even eat these patties on rolls with pasta sauce and mozzarella for a great zucchini sandwich. Or layer them like eggplant in a casserole dish to make a tasty zucchini patty Parmesan. Yum!

2 to 4 zucchini
2 eggs
1/2 c. all-purpose flour
1/2 c. Italian-seasoned dry
   bread crumbs
2 T. grated Parmesan cheese

1/2 t. Italian seasoning
1/4 c. olive oil
salt and pepper to taste
Optional: pasta sauce or
   sour cream

Shred zucchini using the larger holes of a grater; set aside. In a large bowl, beat eggs well. Add zucchini, flour, bread crumbs, Parmesan cheese and seasonings. Mix well and let stand for 20 minutes. Heat a skillet over medium heat; add olive oil. Add zucchini mixture by tablespoonfuls; flatten each slightly with a fork. Cook patties on both sides until golden. Remove to a plate lined with paper towels; drain. Serve warm, garnished with pasta sauce or sour cream, if desired. Serves 4 to 6.

Enjoy a taste of summer in fall. Make an extra of a favorite veggie casserole to tuck in the freezer. Wrap well with plastic wrap and freeze. To serve, thaw overnight in the refrigerator and bake as usual.

Baked Acorn Squash
with Cinnamon Apples

Marsha Baker
Pioneer, OH

A friend shared this delightful recipe with me and I love it!
I can make a meal of this delicious squash.

2 to 3 acorn squash
2 to 3 apples, cored and diced
1/2 c. light brown sugar, packed
1/4 c. butter, melted

1 T. all-purpose flour
1/2 t. salt
1-1/2 t. pumpkin pie spice
1/2 to 3/4 c. water

Halve squash; clean out seeds and stringy pulp. Arrange halves cut-side up in an ungreased 13"x9" baking pan; fill with apples and set aside. In a small bowl, stir together brown sugar, butter, flour and seasonings. Drizzle over squash. Pour water into pan around squash. Cover pan with aluminum foil. Bake at 350 degrees for 60 to 70 minutes, until squash and apples are tender. Cool for several minutes before serving. Makes 6 to 8 servings.

Hard-shelled squash can be hard to cut open. Do it the easy way, in the microwave! Cook the whole squash on high setting for 5 minutes. Pierce with a knife tip to check for tenderness and cook a few more minutes, as needed. Cool, cut in half and scoop out the seeds...ready for your recipe.

Donna's Scalloped Sweet Potatoes

Donna Wilson
Maryville, TN

This is a favorite for my family at Thanksgiving get-togethers.
We love it, so I try to make it more often than once a year.

4 sweet potatoes, peeled and
    thinly sliced
4 slices bacon
1 onion, chopped
2 T. all-purpose flour
2 c. milk

2 c. shredded mozzarella cheese,
    divided
salt and pepper to taste
Optional: 1/2 c. shredded
    Parmesan cheese

Bring a large saucepan of water to a boil over high heat. Add sweet potato slices. Cook for 5 minutes, or until softened; drain. Meanwhile, in a skillet over medium heat, cook bacon until crisp. Remove bacon to a paper towel; reserve drippings in skillet. Add onion to drippings over low heat. Stir in flour until a paste forms; gradually add milk, 1-1/2 cups mozzarella cheese and seasonings. Cook and stir until mixture thickens. In a greased 13"x9" baking pan, arrange half each of sweet potatoes, crumbled bacon and cheese sauce. Repeat layers; top with remaining mozzarella cheese and Parmesan cheese, if using. Bake, uncovered, at 325 degrees for 20 minutes, or until bubbly. Serves 8.

When we moved to Arizona from Washington state 15 years ago, I was not prepared for the change in seasons and environment. Fall came and I was so sad not to be able to enjoy the fall leaves and beautiful colors in the northwest. So I decided to start a new tradition. Every October, I get out our faux Christmas tree and decorate it for fall with orange lights and colorful fall leaves. My family & friends loved it! Every year they ask me "When is your fall tree coming out?" We're back in Washington now and I still decorate my fall tree.

–Amy Delorme, Bellingham, WA

Harvest Corn Casserole

Cindy Rocco
Danbury, CT

This tasty recipe is part of our family tradition...it just wouldn't be Thanksgiving without it. Then on Black Friday morning, before the sun comes up, while others are shopping for bargains, I begin making turkey soup. While the soup bubbles away, I heat some leftover corn casserole and drizzle it with maple syrup...yum!

2 8-1/2 oz. pkgs. corn muffin
   mix
1/2 c. butter, melted
16-oz. container sour cream

2 14-3/4 oz. cans creamed corn
2 15-oz. cans corn
1 egg, slightly beaten

Combine all ingredients in a large bowl; stir until blended. Pour into a buttered 13"x9" baking pan. Bake, uncovered, at 350 degrees for 45 minutes to one hour, until top is lightly golden. Makes 10 to 12 servings.

Pepper Jack Scalloped Corn

Lindsey Chrostowski
Janesville, WI

This is a must for our Thanksgiving and Christmas dinners!

14-3/4 oz. can creamed corn
1 egg, beaten
1 c. milk
2 T. butter, melted
1 t. pepper

22 round buttery crackers,
   crushed
6-oz. pkg. shredded Pepper Jack
   cheese

Combine all ingredients in a bowl; stir well. Pour into an ungreased 2-quart casserole dish. Bake, uncovered, at 350 degrees for about one hour. Makes 4 to 6 servings.

I awoke this morning with devout thanksgiving
for my friends, the old and new.

–Ralph Waldo Emerson

Southwest Hominy & Corn Casserole

Betty Kozlowski
Newnan, GA

I found this wonderful recipe in a vegetarian cookbook and made it my own, adding green chiles and Pepper Jack cheese for a southwest flavor. The bacon just puts it over the top! To serve as a vegetarian main dish, simply omit the bacon and double the cheese.

2 15-1/2 oz. cans white
   hominy, drained
4 c. frozen corn, thawed
7-oz. can chopped green chiles

1 c. shredded Pepper Jack cheese
6 to 8 slices bacon, crisply
   cooked and crumbled

Combine hominy, corn and chiles in a large bowl; mix well. Spray a 4-quart slow cooker with non-stick vegetable spray. Layer 1/3 each of hominy mixture and cheese in slow cooker. Repeat layers 2 more times. Top with crumbled bacon. Cover and cook on high setting for one hour. Reduce to low setting; cook for 3 to 5 hours. Makes 10 to 12 servings.

Dress up plain pillar candles in an instant...press in
white ball-headed straight pins or brass upholstery tacks
to form spirals, stars or simple words.

Ruby's Thanksgiving Cornbread Dressing

Carla McRorie
Kannapolis, NC

My mother-in-law taught me how to make her dressing, thankfully, or else the recipe would be lost. The cornbread needs to be made the night before. I usually end up making two recipes of the cornbread, because everyone wants to eat hot cornbread with butter as soon as it comes out of the oven!

1 onion, diced
2 stalks celery, diced
2 T. dried sage, or more
   to taste

pepper to taste
1 to 1-1/2 c. turkey pan juices
   or canned chicken broth
Optional: salt to taste

Make Cornbread the night before; set aside. Up to 2 hours before serving time, crumble cornbread into a large bowl. Add onion, celery, sage and pepper; stir. Add the juices from turkey roasting pan into mixture as they become available, or add enough chicken broth to make mixture very moist, but not soggy. Season with salt, if needed. Let stand until 30 minutes before serving time. Spoon dressing into a greased cast-iron skillet. Do not fill to the rim; make a second small pan if needed. Smooth top. Bake, uncovered, at 400 degrees for 30 minutes. Serves 8.

Cornbread:

1/2 c. shortening
2 c. yellow cornmeal
1 T. baking powder

2 eggs, beaten
1-1/4 c. buttermilk
3 T. all-purpose flour

Place shortening in a cast-iron skillet; place in a 400-degree oven to melt while preheating. Combine cornmeal and baking powder in a bowl; set aside. In a separate bowl, whisk together eggs and buttermilk; add to cornmeal mixture and stir well. Remove hot skillet from oven. Pour hot shortening into batter; stir well. Shake flour into skillet, like flouring a cake pan; add batter. Bake at 400 degrees for 30 minutes, or until golden.

Salads & Sides

Ginny's Turkey Dressing

Sheri Kohl
Wentzville, MO

As a young newlywed hundred of miles from home, my mom asked the butcher at the local grocery store how to make turkey dressing (never stuffing!) for her first Thanksgiving with my dad. She modified the recipe over the years, but I've never had any other dressing that can beat this family favorite.

24-oz. loaf white sandwich bread	1/2 c. celery, thinly sliced
1 lb. ground pork sausage	3 T. poultry seasoning
1 lb. ground beef	2 T. dried sage
4 eggs, beaten	1/2 t. salt
1 onion, chopped	pepper to taste
	2 c. boiling water

One to 2 days ahead of time, place bread slices on baking sheets. Place on countertop or in turned-off oven to dry. Break bread into bite-sized pieces; place in a very large bowl. Add uncooked sausage, uncooked beef and remaining ingredients except boiling water; toss to mix. Pour boiling water over all; mix thoroughly. Transfer to a lightly greased 13"x9" baking pan. Bake, uncovered, at 350 degrees for one to 1-1/2 hours. Makes 8 to 10 servings.

One Thanksgiving we were having our new house built and couldn't have the family over for dinner. So one of my nieces said she could host it at her house. We took over the turkeys and the dishes we always made. My niece was making sweet potatoes with marshmallows on the top. She put them in the oven to melt the marshmallows. I heard her say something was wrong with her oven, as the marshmallows were not melting. I asked her some questions about her oven. My husband looked at me and mouthed, "Leave her alone, she knows her own oven." About that time, she said, "Look!" and pulled out the bottom of her stove. She had put the dish in the drawer, not the broiler part of the stove!

–Judy Beaty, St. Peters, MO

Loaded Mashed Cauliflower

Lisa Shroyer
Niles, MI

This is delish! I found a similar recipe using potatoes. After being diagnosed with diabetes, I decided to lighten it up by using cauliflower. It's even tastier the next day.

1 head cauliflower, chopped
1/2 c. light sour cream
1/2 c. light mayonnaise
salt and pepper to taste
3 green onions, thinly sliced

8-oz. pkg. shredded sharp
   Cheddar cheese
8 slices bacon, crisply cooked,
   crumbled and divided

Add cauliflower to a saucepan of boiling water. Boil until tender-crisp; drain. Meanwhile, in a bowl, combine sour cream, mayonnaise, salt and pepper. In a large bowl, combine cooked cauliflower, onions and cheese. Add bacon, reserving a small amount to sprinkle on top. Add sour cream mixture; stir well to combine. Lightly spray a 13"x9" glass baking pan with non-stick vegetable spray. Spoon mixture into pan; sprinkle with reserved bacon. Bake, uncovered, at 350 degrees for 20 to 25 minutes, until bubbly and cheese is melted. Makes 10 to 12 servings.

The weekend before Thanksgiving, invite a friend over to make ahead a few harvest dishes for the big day. You can even trade specialties, such as her nut bread for your special spiced apples. While you're chatting and laughing together, you'll be done in no time!

Salads & Sides

Tena's Holiday Rice

Tena Huckleby
Morristown, TN

My family likes rice and I cook it often. Whenever I do, I make a large quantity and refrigerate the extra. This recipe using leftover rice is easy to prepare. The olives give it a special flavor.

1/4 c. butter
2 c. cooked rice
1/2 c. fresh or canned tomato, diced
1/4 c. celery, chopped
1/3 c. onion, chopped

1/4 c. chopped green olives with pimentos
1 T. fresh parsley, chopped
1 t. salt
1 t. pepper

Melt butter in a large non-stick skillet over medium heat. Add cooked rice; cook and stir until rice softens. Reduce heat to low. Add remaining ingredients and simmer for 10 minutes. Makes 6 to 8 servings.

Dilled Peas & Mushrooms

Kathy Courington
Canton, GA

My husband is not fond of peas, but he likes this easy side dish.

1/2 c. onion, finely chopped
2 c. frozen peas, thawed
4-oz. can sliced mushrooms

1/2 t. dried dill weed
Optional: 2-oz. jar chopped pimentos

In a skillet sprayed with non-stick vegetable spray, sauté onion over medium heat for 5 minutes. Add peas, mushrooms with liquid, dill weed and pimentos with liquid, if using. Mix well and cover. Reduce heat to low. Simmer for 5 minutes, or until heated through. Makes 4 to 6 servings.

A delicious drizzle for steamed veggies!
Boil 1/2 cup balsamic vinegar, stirring often,
until thickened. So simple and scrumptious.

Roasted Garlic Twice-Baked Potatoes

Amanda Hettinger
Kirkwood, MO

This is our favorite side dish for steak! The roasted garlic and buttermilk combination adds delicious flavor, while keeping this recipe much lighter than traditional twice-baked potatoes.

4 baking potatoes
1/4 c. butter, softened
1/2 c. buttermilk
1/2 c. low-fat milk

1-1/2 t. fresh thyme, chopped, or 1/2 t. dried thyme
salt and pepper to taste

Scrub potatoes; pierce skins with a fork. Bake at 400 degrees for one hour, or until fork-tender. Meanwhile, prepare Roasted Garlic; add to oven with potatoes during last 40 minutes of baking time. Remove potatoes and garlic from oven; turn oven to 425 degrees. Slice each potato in half and carefully scoop out potato pulp into a bowl, creating potato shells. Squeeze roasted garlic over pulp; mash with butter, milks and thyme. Season with salt and pepper. Carefully stuff potato mixture back into potato skins; place on a baking sheet. Bake, uncovered, for 20 to 25 minutes. Makes 4 to 8 servings.

Roasted Garlic:

2 heads garlic
olive oil to taste

salt and pepper to taste

Slice off the top of each head of garlic just enough to expose the tops of the cloves. Drizzle olive oil, salt and pepper over garlic; wrap each head tightly in aluminum foil. Bake at 400 degrees for 40 minutes.

Be Thankful

There is always something for which to be thankful.

–Charles Dickens

Bleenies Potato Pancakes

Patti Bogetti
Magnolia, DE

*Whenever I make these, it brings back memories of the summers my
brother & I would spend at our grandparents' house in the coal
region of Pennsylvania. They would take us to the church bazaar
so we could wait in line to purchase these delicious crispy pancakes.*

1 c. all-purpose flour
2 t. baking powder
1 t. salt
1/8 t. pepper
2 eggs, beaten

1 c. milk
1/4 c. margarine, melted
2 T. onion, grated
3 c. uncooked potatoes, grated
oil for frying

In a small bowl, mix flour, baking powder, salt and pepper; set aside.
In a large bowl, beat together eggs, milk, margarine and onion until
combined. Add flour mixture to milk mixture; stir well. Fold in the
grated potatoes. Heat 1/2-inch oil in a large skillet over medium heat.
Drop potato mixture into oil by heaping 1/4 cupfuls; press to flatten.
Cook about 3 to 4 minutes on each side, until crisp and golden. Drain
on paper towels. Makes 6 to 8 servings.

Winter is on the way...get ready by making some super-easy
fire-starters to fill a basket by the hearth. Fold sheets of newspaper
into small squares and tie package-style with kitchen string. To
use, tuck a square under the firewood and light with a match.

Tasty Fall Cooking

Spinach-Cheese Casserole

Delores Lakes
Mansfield, OH

Everyone loves this yummy casserole and asks for the recipe. At holidays, it is always on the table and everyone expects to see it there!

2 10-oz. pkgs. frozen chopped
    spinach, thawed
10-3/4 oz. can cream of
    mushroom soup
2 eggs, lightly beaten

1 c. mayonnaise
1 c. shredded Cheddar cheese
1/4 c. onion, chopped
salt and pepper to taste

Drain spinach very well, squeezing out all the moisture. Combine spinach and remaining ingredients in a buttered 2-quart casserole dish; mix well. Bake, uncovered, at 350 degrees for 45 minutes, or until a knife tip inserted in the center comes out clean. Makes 8 servings.

We often decorate our mantels, but why not show off your favorites around the hearth? Candles tucked in tiny terra-cotta pots, punched tin lanterns, bunches of Indian corn or wheat and plump pumpkins look pretty grouped together in a cozy corner.

134

Salads & Sides

Green Beans with Bacon-Balsamic Vinaigrette

Becky Butler
Keller, TX

I love to use whole green beans in this dish because they seem fancier than cut green beans. By the time the beans have finished steaming in the microwave, your sauce is usually completed and you're ready to serve!

2 lbs. whole fresh or frozen
    green beans
1/4 c. water
4 slices bacon
1/4 c. onion or shallots, minced

1/4 c. almonds, coarsely
    chopped
1-1/2 to 2 T. brown sugar,
    packed
1/4 c. white balsamic vinegar

Place green beans in a microwave-safe dish; add water. Cover and microwave on high for 6 minutes, or until crisp-tender and still bright green. Drain well; place green beans on a serving platter and set aside. Cook bacon in a small skillet over medium-high heat until crisp. Remove bacon from skillet; crumble and set aside. Add onion or shallots to drippings in skillet; sauté for one minute. Add almonds; sauté for one minute. Remove from heat; let cool slightly. Add vinegar and brown sugar to skillet; cook and stir until sugar dissolves. Add crumbled bacon; stir well. Pour hot mixture over beans; toss gently to coat. Makes 8 servings.

Fall fun! Take the kids to a neighborhood garden center for all-you-can-carry pumpkins, shiny gourds, corn shocks for the porch posts and maybe even a cup of fresh cider. While you're there, pick out some daffodil bulbs to plant in October.

Baked Cranberries

Mary Ann McGrath
Lawrenceburg, KY

*I received this recipe from a dear friend of my parents
who lived in Alabama.*

12-oz. pkg. fresh cranberries
1 c. sugar

1 c. broken pecan pieces
8-oz. jar orange marmalade

Place cranberries in a shallow one-quart casserole dish; sprinkle with
sugar. Cover with aluminum foil. Bake at 325 degrees for one hour.
During the last 10 minutes of the baking hour, spread pecans on a
baking sheet; toast in the oven with the cranberries. At the end of
one full hour, remove from oven. Stir pecans and marmalade into
cranberries. Serve hot or cold. Makes 10 to 12 servings.

Apple Kugel

Diane Himpelmann
Ringwood, IL

*I have a family of meat eaters, vegetarians and folks on special
diets. It is hard to make something for all. So I made this up
from several ideas. It was a hit...there were no leftovers!*

4 c. thin egg noodles, uncooked
3 apples, peeled, cored and
   thinly sliced
3 T. olive oil

1 t. cinnamon, or to taste
3 eggs, lightly beaten
8-oz. can crushed pineapple,
   well drained

Cook noodles according to package directions; drain. Meanwhile,
in a skillet over medium heat, sauté apples in oil. Drain; sprinkle with
cinnamon. Add eggs, pineapple and noodles; mix well. Spoon into a
greased 3-quart casserole dish. Bake, uncovered, at 350 degrees for
one hour. Serves 4.

If it's Thanksgiving now, Christmas can't be far away. Why not
double any festive side dishes and freeze half for Christmas
dinner...you'll be so glad you did!

Bountiful Autumn Dinners

Garlic Grilled Chicken & Zucchini

Christy Young
North Attleboro, MA

I love this tender juicy chicken! Add some grilled zucchini and a baked potato and you have a magnificent meal on a sunny fall day. Add a few yellow summer squash too, if you like. Delicious!

4 boneless, skinless chicken
   breasts
1/2 c. catsup
1/4 c. cider vinegar

1 T. lemon juice
1 T. garlic, minced
salt and pepper to taste

Place chicken in a large plastic zipping bag; set aside. Combine remaining ingredients in a small bowl; mix well and pour over chicken. Seal bag; turn to coat chicken. Refrigerate for about one hour before grilling. Drain, discarding marinade. Place chicken on a grill over over medium-high heat. Grill for about 6 minutes on each side, until golden and chicken juices run clear when pierced. Serves 4.

Grilled Zucchini:

2 to 3 zucchini, sliced
1 T. olive oil
1 clove garlic, minced

garlic powder, salt and pepper
   to taste

Combine all ingredients in a plastic zipping bag; mix well. Transfer vegetables to a grilling basket. Grill for about 20 minutes, turning once or twice, until tender.

Make mini wreaths of rosemary to slip around dinner napkins.
Simply wind fresh rosemary stems into a ring shape, tuck in
the ends and tie on a tiny bow...so pretty!

Autumn Dinners

Maple-Mustard Chicken

JoAnn

Everyone loves this sweet and savory chicken! Sometimes I slice boneless chicken thighs into strips to marinade and grill, then serve them as appetizers. If it's too chilly to grill, the broiler works fine.

8 bone-in chicken thighs,
   skin removed
1/3 c. spicy brown mustard
2 T. yellow mustard
3 T. maple syrup
2 T. brown sugar, packed

1 T. onion, grated
1 T. cider vinegar
2 t. soy sauce
1 clove garlic, minced
1/4 t. salt
1/2 t. pepper

Place chicken in a large plastic zipping bag; set aside. Mix remaining ingredients in a bowl. Add half of marinade to chicken in bag; reserve remaining marinade. Add chicken to bag; seal. Refrigerate chicken and reserved marinade. Chill for 30 minutes to 2 hours. Coat grill rack with non-stick vegetable spray; preheat grill to medium-high heat. Arrange chicken on grill, discarding marinade in bag. Grill for about 8 minutes on each side, until golden and chicken juices run clear. Serve chicken with reserved marinade on the side. Makes 8 servings.

Sometimes you just have to laugh! The first year my husband and I were married, I hosted the holidays at our house. Well. Apparently, a good turkey is in the details!

1. Remove junk inside before cooking.
2. Stuffing said bird to roast is tricky...and NOT recommended!
3. When said bird is done, its drumsticks will come off really easily! Making said bird too ugly to present on a platter!
4. Relax...it all eats the same!

–LeAnn Manes, Broken Arrow, OK

Scott's Baked Beans & Pork Chops

Ramona Wysong
Barlow, KY

This is my brother Scott's recipe. He likes to play around with dishes. This dish has some heat from the hot sauce, but if you like things really spicy, substitute a tiny dash of habanero sauce.

28-oz. can baked beans with
    onions
16-oz. can baked beans with
    onions
1/2 c. onion, chopped
1/2 c. green pepper, chopped

1/4 c. Dijon mustard
2 T. Worcestershire sauce
1 T. hot cayenne pepper sauce
6 boneless pork chops,
    1 inch thick

Combine both cans of beans and remaining ingredients except pork chops in an ungreased shallow 3-quart casserole dish. Mix well. Arrange pork chops over bean mixture, turning chops once to coat with sauce. Bake, uncovered, at 400 degrees for 30 to 40 minutes, until pork chops are no longer pink in the center. Stir beans once or twice during baking, to prevent them from drying out. Makes 6 servings.

Dress up the dinner table with "pumpkins" made of bright orange chrysanthemums. Trim the stems of real or silk mums to one inch and insert the stems into a large styrofoam ball until it's completely covered. Add a cluster of green leaves at the top for the pumpkin "stem." Balance several pumpkin balls atop stemmed glasses... so eye-catching!

Italian Sausage & Potato Roast

Diane Cohen
Breinigsville, PA

*So easy..everything is baked on a sheet pan! I've made this
with turkey sausage and it was delicious too.*

3/4 lb. redskin potatoes, cut into
   quarters
1 yellow pepper, sliced into
   strips
1 green pepper, sliced into strips
1/2 sweet onion, sliced

1 T. olive oil
1 t. garlic salt or garlic powder
1/4 t. dried oregano
pepper to taste
1 lb. Italian pork sausage,
   cut into chunks

In a large bowl, toss vegetables with olive oil and seasonings. Line
a large rimmed baking sheet with aluminum foil; lightly mist with
non-stick vegetable spray. Spread vegetables on baking sheet. Place
sausage chunks among vegetables. Bake, uncovered, at 450 degrees
until sausage is cooked through and vegetables are tender, about
30 minutes, stirring twice during baking. Makes 4 servings.

Italian-Style Garlic Butter

Leona Krivda
Belle Vernon, PA

*This is a great spread for bread! It's nice that you can
keep it in the fridge, ready to go with a tasty dinner.*

1/2 c. butter, softened
1/4 c. mayonnaise
2 T. grated Parmesan cheese

1 t. dried basil
1/2 t. dried oregano
1 clove garlic, minced

In a bowl, beat all ingredients with an electric mixer on medium speed
until blended. Cover; refrigerate up to one month. To serve: Halve a
loaf of French bread. Spread mixture over cut sides of loaf. Add top
half of loaf; wrap in aluminum foil. Bake at 350 degrees for 10 minutes.
May also spread on slices of French bread. Broil 4 inches from heat
2 to 3 minutes, until golden. Makes 3/4 cup.

Confetti Spaghetti

Cyndy DeStefano
Mercer, PA

This is a comfort food at our house. It is a perfect Saturday meal because you can cook the chicken early in the day and then put the casserole together at dinnertime. Serve with a big tossed salad and crusty rolls.

2 chicken breasts, skin removed
16-oz. pkg. thin spaghetti,
   uncooked and broken in half
 2 10-3/4 oz. cans cream of
   mushroom soup
1/2 c. onion, finely diced
4-oz. jar diced pimentos, drained

1 c. mushrooms, diced
1 green pepper, finely diced
8-oz. pkg. shredded Monterey
   Jack cheese, divided
1/4 t. cayenne pepper
salt and pepper to taste

Cover chicken with water in a large stockpot over high heat; bring to a boil. Reduce heat to medium-low. Simmer until chicken is done, about 30 minutes. Remove chicken to a plate to cool, reserving broth in stockpot. Skim broth; set aside 2 cups broth. Bring remaining broth in stockpot back to a boil. Add spaghetti and cook according to package directions; drain. In a large bowl, combine soup, vegetables and 1-1/2 cups cheese; mix well. Cut chicken into bite-size pieces. Add chicken and reserved 2 cups broth; mix again. Fold in cooked spaghetti. Season with cayenne pepper, salt and pepper. Transfer mixture to a greased 2-quart casserole dish; top with reserved cheese. Bake, uncovered, at 350 degrees for 35 to 45 minutes. Makes 6 to 8 servings.

For a zippy lemon salad dressing, shake up 1/2 cup olive oil, 1/3 cup fresh lemon juice and a tablespoon of Dijon mustard in a small jar and chill to blend.

Autumn Dinners

Busy-Day Cheesy Pasta

Wendy Paffenroth
Pine Island, NY

Very cheesy and good...terrific for family meals and church suppers. A dash of balsamic vinegar gives pasta great flavor. This can be made up to 3 months ahead and frozen until you have a busy day. Then thaw overnight and bake it for dinner. Serve with hot garlic bread and a fresh tossed salad.

16-oz. pkg. ziti or penne pasta, uncooked
balsamic vinegar to taste
1 lb. sweet Italian pork sausage
1 lb. ground beef
3/4 c. onion, chopped
4 cloves garlic, pressed

29-oz. cans crushed tomatoes
1 c. red wine or beef broth
1 T. sugar
1 T. Italian seasoning
2 to 3 8-oz. pkgs. shredded Cheddar cheese

Cook pasta according to package directions; drain. Add a splash of balsamic vinegar; stir to coat pasta and set aside. While pasta is cooking, boil sausage in a large pot of water. Drain; rinse sausage under cold water and cut into 1/2-inch slices. Transfer sausage slices to a stockpot; cook over medium heat until golden. Add beef, onion and garlic to sausage; cook until beef is browned and onion is tender. Stir in tomatoes with juice, wine or beef broth, sugar and seasonings. Simmer until blended, adding a little more wine or broth if too thick. Spread a little of mixture in the bottom of a greased 3-quart casserole dish. Layer half the pasta, half of the remaining sauce and half the cheese. Repeat layering. Bake, uncovered, at 325 degrees for about 40 minutes, until hot and bubbly. Makes 6 servings.

For baked casseroles, cook pasta for the shortest cooking time recommended on the package. It's not necessary to rinse the cooked pasta...just drain it well.

New Mexico Green Chile Turkey Stacked Enchiladas

Darcy Obar
Tonopah, NV

I didn't know what a green chile was until I married into a family from New Mexico! My mother-in-law made this delicious enchilada-style casserole and it was so delicious! Creamy, cheesy, spicy goodness! Make it as hot or mild as you like. I use Hatch green chiles from New Mexico because of their distinctive flavor and heat. Serve with pinto beans and Mexican rice for a wonderful hearty meal.

10-3/4 oz. can cream of
    mushroom soup
10-3/4 oz. cream of chicken
    soup
10-3/4 oz. Cheddar cheese soup
2-1/2 c. milk or whipping cream
garlic powder, salt and pepper to
    taste
4 c. shredded cooked turkey

16-oz. container frozen green
    chiles, thawed, or 4 4-oz.
    cans diced chiles
24 8-inch corn tortillas, warmed
    and divided
16-oz. pkg. shredded Colby Jack
    cheese, divided
Garnish: sour cream, sliced black
    olives

In a large saucepan, combine soups, milk or cream, green chiles and seasonings. Simmer over low heat until heated through. Stir in turkey and chiles; heat through. Spray a 13"x9" baking pan with non-stick vegetable spray. Spread a thin layer of soup mixture in bottom of pan. Place 6 warmed tortillas over sauce to cover bottom of pan. Cover tortillas with 1/4 of remaining soup mixture and 1/4 of cheese; add 6 more tortillas. Repeat layering, ending with soup and cheese. Bake, uncovered, at 350 degrees for 30 minutes, or until bubbly and golden. Top with sour cream and black olives. Serves 6.

To warm tortillas, wrap tortillas in paper towels, 6 at a time, and microwave for 30 seconds. Or warm them on a hot griddle.

Cozy Potato Burritos

Andrea Heyart
Savannah, TX

*I love this hearty recipe in the fall. It's warm and spicy...
the potato really makes it stick to your ribs. Or slice these
burritos pinwheel-style and serve them as tasty appetizers.*

1 lb. ground beef
1 russet potato, peeled and
   shredded
3 green onions, diced, both
   green and white parts
15-oz. can diced tomatoes,
   drained
4-oz. can diced green chiles

1 T. garlic, minced
salt and pepper to taste
10 10-inch flour tortillas
16-oz. pkg. shredded Cheddar
   cheese
Optional: 1/4 c. fresh cilantro,
   chopped
Garnish: sour cream

Brown beef in a large skillet over medium heat. Drain; add potato,
onions, tomatoes, chiles, garlic, salt and pepper. Cook over medium
heat for about 15 minutes, stirring often, until potato is soft and
tender. Remove from heat. For each burrito, cover one tortilla with
cheese; spoon some of beef mixture down the center. Top with
cilantro, if desired. Roll up tightly; repeat with remaining ingredients.
Serve with a dollop of sour cream on top. Makes 10 servings.

Bored with leftover turkey sandwiches? Add a barbecue twist!
Sauté some chopped onions in a little butter; stir in cubed turkey
and enough barbecue sauce to coat well. Simmer until heated
through, then spoon onto soft onion rolls and enjoy.

Mississippi Pot Roast

Danielle Dorward
San Diego, CA

I don't know how this recipe got its name, but I do know it's delicious. Served over fluffy mashed potatoes, it's the perfect autumn comfort meal with very little effort on your part.

3-lb. beef chuck roast
1-oz. pkg. ranch salad dressing
   mix
1-oz. pkg. au jus mix
1/2 c. butter, sliced
6 to 8 pepperoncini peppers,
   stems removed

1 to 2 T. pepperoncini juice
1-1/2 c. mushrooms, halved
   or quartered
3 to 4 carrots, peeled and sliced
   into large pieces, or 1/2 lb.
   baby carrots
mashed potatoes

Place roast in a 6-quart slow cooker. Sprinkle dry mixes over roast. Place butter on top of roast. Add pepperoncinis; drizzle pepperoncini juice over roast. Cover and cook on low setting for 4 hours; turn the roast over. Cover and cook for another hour. Add mushrooms and carrots; cover and cook for 2 to 3 more hours, or until roast is very tender. Slightly shred roast. Serve with vegetables over mashed potatoes, topped with some of the gravy from slow cooker.
Serves 4 to 6.

Are you hosting a big dinner gathering? Set out all the serving platters, baskets and dishes ahead of time and tag them. When the time arrives, you'll be able to put dinner on the table in a jiffy.

Bountiful
Autumn Dinners

Cheeseburger Pie Supreme

Cheryl Culver
Perkins, OK

If you love cheeseburgers, this pie will make you love them even more! It makes a big hit at potlucks and family get-togethers.

1 lb. lean ground beef
1 large onion, chopped
1 lb. sliced mushrooms
4-oz. can sliced black olives,
　　drained
1/2 t. garlic powder

1/2 t. seasoned salt
1/8 t. Worcestershire sauce
1 c. shredded Cheddar cheese
2 eggs, beaten
1 c. milk
1/2 c. biscuit baking mix

In a skillet over medium heat, cook beef, onion, mushrooms and olives for about 10 minutes, until beef is browned. Drain; stir in garlic powder, salt and Worcestershire sauce. Spread beef mixture in a 9" pie plate sprayed with non-stick vegetable spray. Sprinkle cheese over top; set aside. In a small bowl, whisk together eggs, milk and baking mix until as smooth as possible. Pour batter over beef mixture. Bake, uncovered, at 400 degrees for 25 minutes, or until a knife tip comes out clean. Cut into wedges. Serves 4 to 6.

Savor a warm autumn evening by toting supper to the backyard. Kids can work up an appetite before dinner playing Tag or Hide-and-Seek. Afterwards, what could be better for dessert than marshmallows toasted over a fire ring?

Harvest Chicken with Thyme, Beets & Onions

Mary Thomason-Smith
Bloomington, IN

Browned in a skillet and finished in the oven, these succulent chicken breasts make a fast dinner that tastes like it roasted all afternoon. Just add a tossed green salad for a colorful harvest celebration.

4 chicken breasts
2 cloves garlic, slivered
salt and pepper to taste
1 T. butter
3 T. olive oil, divided

4 to 6 beets, peeled and
   quartered
2 sweet onions, peeled and
   quartered
Garnish: chopped fresh thyme

Carefully loosen skin on chicken breasts; place slivers of garlic underneath skin. Season chicken with salt and pepper. Melt butter with one tablespoon olive oil in a skillet over medium heat. Place chicken in skillet, skin-side down. Cook over medium-high heat for 3 minutes, or until skin is golden. Place chicken skin-side up in a lightly greased 13"x9" baking pan; set aside. Coat beets and onions in remaining oil; season with salt and pepper. Arrange beets and onions around chicken breasts. Bake, uncovered, at 450 degrees for 30 minutes, or until chicken juices run clear when pierced with a knife. Remove from oven; cover with aluminum foil and let stand for 10 minutes. Arrange chicken, beets and onions on a platter; sprinkle with thyme. Serves 4.

Try a new side dish tonight...barley pilaf. Simply prepare quick-cooking barley with chicken broth instead of water, seasoning it with a little sautéed onion and parsley. Filling, quick and tasty!

Autumn Dinners

Bar-B-Q Chicken Veggie Stir-Fry

Audrey Kleespies
Alexandria, MN

You can eat a plate full of this yummy recipe with no guilt!
Serve on a pretty plate with a bread stick on the side, if you
like. It has a bite from the barbecue sauce and is delicious!

3/4 c. cooked chicken, cubed
1 T. spicy barbecue sauce
1 T. safflower or olive oil
Optional: 1 T. onion, minced
2 zucchini, sliced

2 yellow squash, sliced
3/4 c. carrot, peeled and
  shredded
12 sugar peas or snow pea pods,
  coarsely chopped

Toss chicken cubes with barbecue sauce; set aside. In a large skillet,
heat oil over medium-high heat. Add onion, if using; cook until golden.
Add remaining vegetables and chicken mixture. Cook for several
minutes, using a spatula to flip, until mixture is dark golden on the
edges but vegetables remain tender-crisp. Serves 3 to 4.

Country-Style Chicken Dinner

Joyceanne Dreibelbis
Wooster, OH

This is a simple, delicious meal that's perfect for a
Sunday night family get-together or a church potluck.

3 c. frozen diced potatoes
2.8-oz. can French fried onions,
  divided
10-3/4 oz. can cream of chicken
  soup
1 c. milk

6 slices American cheese
2 to 2-1/2 lbs. chicken pieces,
  skin removed if desired
10-oz. pkg. frozen mixed
  vegetables, thawed and
  drained

In a greased 13"x9" baking pan, combine frozen potatoes and 1/2 can
onions. In a bowl, blend soup and milk; spoon half over potato mixture.
Arrange cheese on top. Add chicken, skin-side down, and remaining
soup mixture. Bake, uncovered, at 375 degrees for 35 minutes. Stir
vegetables into potatoes; turn chicken over. Return to oven for
20 minutes, or until chicken is done. Stir; top chicken with remaining
onions. Bake another 3 minutes. Let stand 15 minutes. Serves 6 to 8.

White Tie & Tails

Carolyn Deckard
Bedford, IN

*My sister Linda Lou gave me this recipe for bow tie pasta
and cheese years ago. It's very good. I love the name of
the recipe...it seems so fancy!*

8-oz. pkg. bow tie pasta,
  uncooked
1-1/2 T. butter
1 c. half-and-half
1-1/2 T. all-purpose flour
1/2 c. shredded baby Swiss
  cheese

1/2 c. crumbled blue cheese
1/2 c. grated Romano cheese
3/4 c. sliced black olives
1/4 c. grated Parmesan cheese
1/3 c. prosciutto or deli ham, cut
  into 1/4-inch strips
2 T. fresh basil, chopped

Cook pasta according to package directions; drain. Meanwhile, melt
butter in a saucepan over medium heat. Gradually stir in half-and-half
and flour. Cook, stirring often, for 3 to 5 minutes, until smooth and
slightly thickened. Add all cheeses except Parmesan. Reduce heat;
cook and stir until cheeses are blended and sauce is smooth. Remove
from heat; stir in olives. Ladle sauce over cooked pasta; toss. Sprinkle
with Parmesan cheese, prosciutto or ham and basil. Serve immediately.
Makes 4 servings.

Make a trivet in a jiffy to protect the tabletop from hot dishes.
Simply attach a cork or felt square to the bottom of a large
ceramic tile with craft glue. It's so easy, why not make several?

Autumn Dinners

Pink Sauce for Pasta

Julie Dossantos
Fort Pierce, FL

This is a great basic homemade pasta sauce. I often add sautéed mushrooms, zucchini and eggplant to this versatile sauce. Serve over your favorite cooked pasta.

1/2 c. cream cheese, cubed
1/2 c. chicken or vegetable broth
3 T. Italian seasoning
1 t. salt
28-oz. can crushed tomatoes
15-oz. can tomato sauce

1 c. fresh basil, coarsely chopped
2 t. sugar
1/2 c. shredded or grated
   Parmesan cheese
1/2 c. whipping cream or milk
pepper to taste

Heat a large saucepan over medium heat; add cream cheese. Stir with a whisk for 2 to 3 minutes, until cheese begins to melt. Slowly whisk in broth, Italian seasoning and salt. Cook and whisk for 2 minutes. Stir in tomatoes with juice, tomato sauce, basil and sugar. Increase heat to medium-high. Cook, uncovered, just until boiling. Reduce heat to medium-low. Cover and simmer, for 10 to 15 minutes. Stir in Parmesan cheese and cream or milk. Season with pepper and additional salt and sugar, as desired. Simmer an additional 5 minutes. Serves 4 to 6.

Whip up a loaf of beer bread for dinner. Combine 2 cups self-rising flour, a 12-ounce can of beer and 3 tablespoons sugar in a greased loaf pan. Bake at 350 degrees for 25 minutes, then drizzle with melted butter. Yum!

Herbed Turkey Breast

June Henson
Roan Mountain, TN

This slow-cooker recipe was given to me some years ago. My family loves it!

5-1/2 to 6-lb. bone-in whole
   turkey breast, thawed
   if frozen
1/2 c. butter
1/4 c. lemon juice
2 T. onion, chopped

2 T. soy sauce
1 T. dried sage
1 t. dried thyme
1 t. dried marjoram
1/4 t. pepper

Pat turkey breast dry; place in a 6-quart slow cooker and set aside. Combine remaining ingredients in a saucepan. Bring to a boil over medium heat; stir well. Brush mixture over turkey breast. Cover and cook on high setting for 4 hours, or on low setting for 8 hours, basting occasionally with drippings. Remove to a platter; let stand several minutes before slicing. Serves 10 to 12.

Dressing, stuffing or filling...whatever you call it, it's better with gravy! Measure 1/4 cup pan drippings into a skillet over medium heat. Stir in 1/4 cup flour. Cook and stir until smooth and bubbly. Add 2 cups skimmed pan juices or canned broth. Cook and stir until boiling. Boil for about one minute, to desired thickness. Add salt and pepper to taste.

Autumn Dinners

Turkey Thyme Tetrazzini

Irene Robinson
Cincinnati, OH

A great way to use leftover roast turkey or chicken!
The thyme is optional, but adds a real flavor boost.

3/4 c. medium egg noodles,
   uncooked
1 T. butter
2 c. sliced mushrooms
1/4 c. light cream cheese spread

1 c. chicken broth
Optional: 1/4 c. fresh thyme,
   chopped, or 1 t. dried thyme
3 c. cooked turkey, cubed
1 c. frozen peas, thawed

Cook noodles according to package directions; drain. Meanwhile, melt butter in a large skillet over medium heat. Add mushrooms; cook until tender. Stir in cream cheese, broth and thyme, if using; bring to a boil. Reduce heat to low. Simmer for 7 minutes, stirring occasionally, or until slightly thickened. Add turkey and peas; cook until heated through. To serve, spoon turkey mixture over noodles. Serves 4.

It was my first family holiday at my Mother & Daddy's home with my boyfriend Jim, shortly before we became engaged. I had never cooked for him and wanted the dinner to be oh-so special. I was a bit nervous but enjoying cooking in the kitchen with Momma while Jim and Daddy watched football in the living room. Finally, the meal was ready and we were putting the meal on the table. I opened the oven, took out the dressing, turned over the bowl...and dropped it on the floor. Momma and I laughed till we had tears. The guys didn't even ask what was going on. I scooped up the top layer (not what touched the floor in her no-pet home) and we served the dressing. To this day when I prepare Thanksgiving dinner for my hubby of 45 years, my Jim, I get tickled at this memory.

–Teresa Golden, Farmersville, TX

Apple-Bacon Pork Chop Pockets

Sarah Olley
Saratoga Springs, NY

I am not usually a pork chop fan, but everyone loved this dish! I used what I had in the kitchen, and the pork chops were so juicy and tender, I surprised myself! Now I am getting requests for this recipe.

4 pork chops, 1 to 2 inches thick
salt and pepper to taste
3 slices bacon, coarsely chopped
1 onion, coarsely chopped
4 fresh basil leaves, chopped
2 t. dried sage
1 Red Delicious apple, peeled,
   cored and very thinly sliced

2 T. butter, room temperature
1 t. cinnamon
1-1/2 c. plus 2 T. orange juice,
   divided
2 to 3 t. oil
1 T. lemon juice
2 t. fresh parsley, chopped,
   or dried parsley

Cut a pocket into one side of each pork chop, pressing your hand firmly on the pork chop to guide the knife. Season pork chops with salt and pepper; set aside. In a large skillet over medium heat, sauté bacon, onion, basil and sage until bacon is slightly crisp and onion begins to caramelize. Transfer mixture to a bowl; add apples, butter, cinnamon and 2 tablespoons orange juice. Stuff pork chop pockets with mixture. Fasten with wooden skewers, if desired. Add oil to the same skillet over medium-high heat. Add pork chops and cook until golden, 4 to 6 minutes per side. In a greased 13"x9" glass baking pan, combine lemon juice and remaining orange juice; add pork chops. Bake, uncovered, at 350 degrees for about 25 minutes, basting 3 times. Remove pork chops to a platter; let stand for 8 minutes. Spoon orange sauce from pan over pork chops before serving. Makes 4 servings.

A baked sweet potato is a delectable fast-fix side. Pierce the potato several times, then bake until tender, about 45 minutes at 400 degrees. Top with butter and a dusting of cinnamon-sugar.

Bacon-Wrapped Pork Tenderloin Patties

Phyl Broich Wessling
Garner, IA

This meal is easy to make, looks great and it always gets compliments. I usually purchase a whole pork tenderloin and slice it myself, or you can ask the butcher to slice it for you.

1 lb. thin-sliced bacon
8 pork tenderloin patties, about
   3/4-inch thick
garlic powder, salt and pepper
   to taste

8 thin slices onion
8 thin slices tomato
8 mushrooms, stems removed
1 T. butter
Garnish: chopped fresh parsley

Criss-cross 2 uncooked bacon slices; place a tenderloin patty on top. Sprinkle with seasonings; top with an onion slice and a tomato slice. Bring bacon slices together, overlapping across the top patty. Repeat with remaining ingredients. Place patties on a broiler rack to catch the drippings. Bake at 350 degrees for 50 to 60 minutes, until bacon is crisp and patties are no longer pink in the center. Shortly before serving time, sauté mushroom caps in butter in a small skillet over medium heat. Use a toothpick to fasten each cap to the center of a tenderloin patty. Arrange patties on a serving platter; garnish with fresh parsley. Makes 8 servings.

Begin a new and heartfelt Thanksgiving tradition. Ask your friends & family to bring a pair of warm mittens or gloves to dinner, then deliver them to your local shelter.

Slow-Cooker Cheesy Chicken Rotini

Tiffany Jones
Locust Grove, AR

I was looking for something I could take to a potluck and decided to tweak a favorite recipe. This is what I came up with...it was a hit!

16-oz. pkg. rotini pasta, uncooked
1 c. cooked chicken, diced
16-oz. pkg. pasteurized process cheese, cubed
2 10-3/4 oz. cans cream of mushroom soup
10-oz. can diced tomatoes with green chiles

4-oz. can mushroom stems & pieces, drained
1/2 c. milk
1/2 c. onion, diced
1 green pepper, diced
1/2 t. salt
1/2 t. pepper

Cook pasta according to package directions; drain. Spray a 5-quart slow cooker with non-stick vegetable spray. Add cooked pasta and remaining ingredients to slow cooker; stir to mix well. Cover and cook on low setting for 2 to 3 hours, until bubbly and cheese is melted. Stir again just before serving. Makes 8 to 10 servings.

Whip up some herb butter to go with hot dinner rolls. To 1/2 cup softened butter, add one tablespoon chopped fresh parsley, 1-1/2 teaspoons minced garlic, one teaspoon Italian seasoning and a squirt of lemon juice. Blend well; wrap and chill before serving.

Slow-Cooker Spicy Cheesy Tortellini

Hilary Stubblebine
Orlando, FL

This recipe is great to enjoy while watching fall football!

1/2 lb. ground beef
1/2 lb. ground spicy pork
   sausage
14-1/2 oz. can diced tomatoes
8-oz. can sliced mushrooms,
   drained

32-oz. jar spaghetti sauce
9-oz. pkg. frozen cheese
   tortellini, uncooked
Garnish: shredded mozzarella
   cheese

Brown beef and sausage in a large skillet over medium heat. Drain; transfer to a 5-quart slow cooker. Add tomatoes with juice, mushrooms and sauce; mix well. Cover and cook on low setting for 3 hours. About 30 minutes before serving, cook tortellini according to package directions; drain and add to mixture in slow cooker. Stir gently. Serve in shallow bowls, topped with mozzarella cheese. Makes 6 servings.

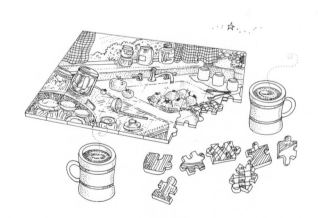

Family night! Serve a simple supper, then spend the chilly evening playing favorite board games or assembling jigsaw puzzles together in front of a toasty fire.

Slow-Cooker Cantonese Dinner

Katie Wollgast
Florissant, MO

This is a recipe my mom used to make. When I was little, I didn't like it because of the peppers, but it has grown to be one of my favorites! I have tweaked it a bit over the years, using a variety of different colored peppers instead of just green ones. If only green are available, the recipe still tastes great, but isn't quite as colorful.

1-1/2 lbs. boneless pork loin, sliced into thin strips
1 to 2 T. oil
1 onion, cut into 1-inch pieces
1 green pepper, cut into 1-inch pieces
1 red pepper, cut into 1-inch pieces
1 yellow pepper, cut into 1-inch pieces
1/2 lb. sliced mushrooms
1 t. salt
1 t. garlic powder
8-oz. can tomato sauce
1 T. Worcestershire sauce
3 T. brown sugar, packed
2 T. vinegar
4 c. hot cooked rice
4 green onions, sliced
1 c. chow mein noodles

In a large skillet over medium heat, brown pork in oil. Drain; transfer to a 5-quart slow cooker. Add onion, peppers, and mushrooms to slow cooker. Sprinkle with salt and garlic powder. Combine tomato sauce, Worcestershire sauce, sugar and vinegar in a small bowl; spoon over vegetables. Cover and cook on low setting for 6 hours, or on high setting for 4 hours. Stir gently; serve over hot cooked rice. Garnish each serving with green onions and chow mein noodles. Makes 4 servings.

The secret to tender steamed rice! Cook long-cooking rice as the package directs. When it's done, uncover the pan, top with a folded tea towel and put the lid back on. Let stand for 5 to 10 minutes before serving. The towel will absorb any excess moisture.

Autumn Dinners

Green Pepper Steak

Dawn Ross
Bemus Point, NY

Use your prettiest large serving platter and garnish with tomato wedges placed around the platter. Your guests will ooh and ahh over the presentation and the flavor of this delicious meal!

1-1/2 lbs. beef flank steak
1/2 c. soy sauce
1 c. water, divided
1 clove garlic, minced
1/4 c. extra-light olive oil
2 green peppers, thinly sliced

1 onion, thinly sliced
3 stalks celery, thinly sliced
   on the diagonal
1 T. cornstarch
steamed rice
Garnish: tomato wedges

Slice steak paper-thin on the diagonal, cutting with the grain of the steak. Place steak in a large bowl; set aside. Combine soy sauce, 1/2 cup water and garlic. Pour mixture over beef; turn to coat slices and let stand for 15 minutes. Drain, reserving marinade. In a wok or skillet over medium-high heat, heat oil until very hot. Brown steak in oil quickly. Push steak to one side of the pan; add green peppers, onion and celery. Cook for 2 minutes, or until vegetable are tender-crisp. Mix reserved marinade and remaining water with cornstarch; stir into steak mixture. Cook and stir until thickened. To serve, ladle beef mixture over hot steamed rice; garnish with tomato wedges. Makes 6 servings.

Cut beef, chicken or pork into thin strips or slices in a snap!
Just pop it in the freezer for 20 to 30 minutes before slicing.

Chicken & Dumplin' Cobbler

Carol Hickman
Kingsport, TN

This cobbler-style casserole is a family favorite. Just add a couple of sides like mashed potatoes and green beans for a quick and tasty weeknight meal.

1/4 c. butter
3 chicken breasts, cooked and cubed, or 2 12-oz. cans chunk chicken breast, drained
2 c. milk

2 c. buttermilk baking mix
10-3/4 oz. can cream of chicken soup
2 to 3 t. poultry seasoning
salt and pepper to taste
3/4 c. chicken broth

Place butter in a 13"x9" baking pan and set in 375-degree oven to melt; remove immediately once butter is melted. Evenly distribute chicken in pan; do not stir. In a bowl, whisk together milk and biscuit mix. Pour batter evenly over chicken; do not stir. To a 2-cup measuring cup, add soup and seasonings. Add enough broth to nearly fill cup; stir gently until blended. Pour soup mixture over batter; do not stir. Bake, uncovered, at 375 degrees for 30 to 40 minutes, until bubbly and top crust is lightly golden. Serves 8.

Need a tiny funnel for filling salt & pepper shakers? Simply cut the corner from a paper envelope, then snip off the tip...perfect!

Sloppy Joe Pie

Beckie Apple
Grannis, AR

*Who doesn't love a big saucy Sloppy Joe! My family loves them
so much I incorporated this favorite into a recipe as a main
dish. It really hits the spot and is quick & easy.*

1-1/2 lbs. ground beef chuck	6-1/2 oz. pkg. cornbread mix
or round	2 eggs, beaten
1/8 t. salt	1/2 c. milk
1/8 t. pepper	2 T. oil
15-1/2 oz. can Sloppy Joe sauce	1/2 c. shredded Cheddar cheese

In a large skillet over medium heat, brown beef; drain and season
with salt and pepper. Add sauce and stir well; simmer for 5 minutes.
Spray an 8"x8" baking pan with non-stick vegetable spray. Spoon
beef mixture into pan and set aside. In a bowl, combine cornbread
mix, eggs, milk and oil; stir until just blended. Spoon cornbread batter
over beef mixture; smooth to edges. Sprinkle cheese on top. Bake,
uncovered, at 375 degrees until golden, about 25 minutes. Makes
6 servings.

Make mealtime extra special with cloth napkins...pretty place
settings too! Simply glue wooden alphabet letter initials
to plain napkin rings.

Million-Dollar Spaghetti

Wendy Quattlebaum
Mcdonough, GA

*I love this dish because the recipe is budget-friendly and goes
a long way. Serve with your favorite bread and enjoy!*

16-oz. pkg. spaghetti, uncooked
1 lb. ground beef or turkey
Optional: 2 t. garlic powder
16-oz. jar spaghetti sauce
8-oz. pkg. cream cheese,
    softened

8-oz. container cottage cheese
1/4 c. sour cream
1/2 c. butter, sliced and divided
8-oz. pkg. shredded Cheddar
    cheese

Cook spaghetti according to package directions; drain. Meanwhile,
brown beef or turkey in a skillet; drain. Add garlic powder, if desired;
stir in spaghetti sauce. Add cream cheese, cottage cheese and sour
cream; cook and stir for 5 to 7 minutes. While sauce is cooking, add
4 sliced tablespoons butter to a 13"x9" baking pan. Layer half of
cooked spaghetti over butter; add half of sauce mixture. Layer with
remaining butter, spaghetti and sauce mixture. Cover with an
aluminum foil tent. Bake at 350 degrees for 30 minutes. Remove foil;
sprinkle with Cheddar cheese. Bake, uncovered, another 10 minutes,
or until cheese is melted. Let stand for 10 minutes before serving.
Makes 8 servings.

If hungry kids are getting underfoot while you're preparing
Thanksgiving dinner, let them make some turkey track snacks!
Spread softened cheese spread on a round buttery cracker
and arrange 3 chow mein noodles on top for the "track."
Place on a platter for tasty nibbling.

Autumn Dinners

Crazy Comforting Spaghetti

Rick Schulte
Wyandotte, MI

*This was by far the quickest and most comforting meal my wife
Tiffani knew how to get onto a plate, and she always had the
ingredients on hand to make it. My son Sam and I could eat it every
day of the week. Tiffani passed away in 2016 at a far-too-young age.
This recipe is shared in her memory.*

1 onion, chopped
1 T. butter
1 T. oil
2 cloves garlic, minced
1-1/2 lbs. ground beef
4 14-oz. cans spaghetti in
    tomato sauce & cheese

1 to 2 T. Worcestershire sauce
1 t. salt
1/2 t. pepper
Garnish: grated Parmesan
    cheese
Optional: hot pepper sauce

In a skillet over medium heat, cook onion in butter and olive oil until
translucent. Add garlic; cook and stir for one minute more. Add beef;
cook until no longer pink. Drain; add spaghetti in sauce, Worcestershire
sauce and seasonings. Heat through. Serve with Parmesan cheese and
hot sauce, if desired. Makes 6 to 8 servings.

An oh-so-easy side to serve with dinner...layer olives, feta cheese
cubes and marinated artichoke hearts in a stemware glass.

Baked Chicken Chimichangas
Linda Diepholz
Lakeville, MN

I have been making these chicken chimis for years. I like that they are baked and not deep-fried...much healthier. People who don't even like Mexican food discover they love these. I make this recipe often and I even like the leftovers cold!

2 c. cooked chicken, chopped
    or shredded
1 c. salsa or picante sauce
2 c. shredded reduced-fat
    Cheddar cheese
4 green onions, chopped

1-1/2 t. ground cumin
1 t. dried oregano
8 8-inch flour tortillas
2 T. light butter, melted
Garnish: additional shredded
    cheese, green onions, salsa

In a bowl, combine chicken, salsa or sauce, cheese, onions and seasonings. Spoon 1/3 cup of mixture down the center of each tortilla; fold opposite sides over filling. Roll up from bottom and place seam-side down on an ungreased baking sheet. Brush with melted butter. Bake, uncovered, at 400 degrees for 30 minutes or until golden, turning halfway through cooking. Garnish with additional cheese and onions; serve with salsa on the side, as desired. Serves 4 to 6.

Chicken & Puff Packages
LaShelle Brown
Mulvane, KS

*My mother used to make these for us kids when we were little.
It was so fun to have our own little packets of food!*

4 boneless, skinless chicken
    breasts
10-3/4 oz. can cream of chicken
    soup

1-1/3 c. frozen mixed vegetables
24 frozen potato puffs

Place each chicken breast on a piece of aluminum foil. Top each with soup to cover, 1/3 cup vegetables and 6 potato puffs. Seal foil tightly. Place on a baking sheet. Bake at 375 degrees for one hour. Makes 4 servings.

Autumn Dinners

Supper Club Enchiladas

Phyl Broich Wessling
Garner, IA

A friend shared this recipe with me. Whenever I prepare it
for guests, they always request the recipe.

1 lb. ground beef
1-1/4 oz. pkg. taco seasoning
   mix
10-3/4 oz. can cream of chicken
   soup
8-oz. container sour cream

4-oz. can diced green chiles
8 8-inch flour tortillas
2 c. shredded Cheddar cheese,
   divided
1 c. green onions, sliced and
   divided

Brown beef in a large skillet over medium heat. Drain; stir in taco
seasoning and simmer another 2 minutes. Remove from heat.
Meanwhile, in a small saucepan over low heat, combine soup, sour
cream and undrained chiles. Cook and stir until bubbly. Set aside
1/2 cup cheese and 1/2 cup green onions. Spread one tablespoon soup
mixture over each tortilla. Top each tortilla with some of beef mixture,
some of remaining cheese and some green onions. Roll up tortillas;
place seam-side down in a greased 3-quart casserole dish. Spoon
remaining soup mixture over top. Cover with aluminum foil. Bake at
350 degrees for 20 minutes, or until bubbly around the edges. Top
with reserved cheese. Bake, uncovered, another 5 minutes. Garnish
with remaining green onions. Serves 4.

Fill a muffin tin with fixings like sliced black olives, chopped
green onions and diced avocado...everyone can top their
own tacos or enchiladas to their liking.

Chicken Garden Medley

Connie McKone
Fort Atkinson, IA

*This is such a great way to use those fresh veggies from
your garden. And it tastes so good too!*

8-oz. pkg. angel hair pasta,
    uncooked
1 lb. boneless, skinless chicken
    breasts, cut into strips
1 clove garlic, minced
1/4 c. butter, divided
1 yellow squash, sliced thin
1 zucchini, sliced thin
1/2 c. green pepper, chopped

1/2 c. red pepper, chopped
1/4 c. onion, sliced
2 T. all-purpose flour
1/2 t. salt
1/4 t. pepper
3/4 c. chicken broth
1/2 c. half-and-half
2 T. grated Parmesan cheese

Cook pasta according to package directions; drain. Meanwhile, in a
skillet over medium heat, sauté chicken and garlic in 2 tablespoons
butter for 10 to 12 minutes, until chicken juices run clear. Add
vegetables; cook until crisp-tender. Transfer chicken mixture to a
2-quart casserole dish. Add pasta; mix gently and set aside. In the
same skillet, melt remaining butter; stir in flour, salt and pepper. Add
chicken broth; cook until thickened. Stir in cream; pour over mixture
in dish. Sprinkle with Parmesan cheese. Bake, covered, at 350 degrees
for 20 minutes; uncover and bake 10 minutes longer. Makes
6 servings.

Chicken backs and wings are excellent for making rich,
delicious broth...a terrific way to use up the last of farm-raised
fowl. Save up unused ones in the freezer until you have
enough for a pot of broth.

Autumn Dinners

Garlic Baked Chicken

Robi Ehrlick
Greeley, CO

My family is trying to eat healthier nowadays. I created this to make eating baked chicken a little more interesting.

2 T. olive oil
1 to 2 cloves garlic, minced
4 boneless, skinless chicken
   breasts
1/3 c. panko bread crumbs

1/4 c. shredded Parmesan
   cheese
1 t. Italian seasoning
pepper to taste

Combine olive oil and garlic in a small microwave-safe cup. Microwave for about 30 seconds, to warm oil and infuse garlic flavor. Brush oil mixture evenly onto chicken breasts; set aside. Combine remaining ingredients in a shallow dish; coat chicken with mixture. Put chicken in a lightly greased 13"x9" baking pan. Bake, uncovered, at 425 degrees for 20 to 30 minutes, until chicken is golden and juices run clear when pierced. Makes 4 servings.

In the early 60s, I was a little girl growing up in the country. We were poor, but as a child I did not realize it. My parents were hard-working people and our home was full of love and the ordinary problems of a family with three children. My sister, ten years older than I, moved to Kansas City after high school. She often brought her city friends home to our quaint farmhouse. One Thanksgiving I remember, we were in the fields cutting milo by hand, which was not fun for us country people. However, our city friends thought it was wonderful! I remember stopping to eat the bountiful Thanksgiving dinner my mom had prepared. We had no dining room, but we all gathered around the kitchen table. I believe moments like those molded me to have the "gather 'round" attitude at my own kitchen table.

–Judy Taylor, Butler, MO

Chicken Curry

Patricia Nau
River Grove, IL

I received this recipe from a college friend 45 years ago.
It's still delicious and easy.

1/2 c. peanut oil
2 10-oz. pkgs. frozen chopped
   onions
2 t. garlic, minced
1 c. water
2 T. soy sauce
2 t. chili powder
1 t. turmeric

1 t. curry powder
1 t. ground ginger
1/2 t. hot pepper sauce
3 lbs. boneless, skinless chicken
   breasts, cut into bite-size
   cubes
cooked rice

In a large saucepan over medium heat, combine oil, onions and garlic. Cook until tender, stirring occasionally. Add remaining ingredients except chicken and rice; mix well. Add chicken; stir to coat. Reduce heat to medium-low. Simmer for 30 to 40 minutes, stirring occasionally, until chicken is very tender. Serve chicken mixture spooned over cooked rice. Makes 6 to 8 servings.

When the kids are studying another country in school, why not try out a meal from that country? Let them help choose a recipe and shop for the ingredients...they'll learn so much and have fun doing it!

Autumn Dinners

Curried Shrimp & Rice

Linda Nielsen
British Columbia, Canada

A friend and former co-worker passed this recipe on to me. Our family has enjoyed it many times in the years since! Add some crusty bread and a crisp tossed salad to round out this satisfying meal. You may use fresh shrimp, but cook them first before adding remaining ingredients.

1 T. oil	2 cloves garlic, minced
1 onion, chopped	1 T. curry powder
14-1/2 oz. can whole or	salt to taste
stewed tomatoes	1 c. brown, basmati or white
1 lb. cooked shrimp, peeled and	long-cooking rice, uncooked
cleaned, thawed if frozen	

Heat oil in a skillet over medium heat. Add onion and cook until golden. Stir in tomatoes with juice; cook until mixture is boiling. Add shrimp, garlic and seasonings; stir well. Reduce heat to low. Cover and cook over medium heat for 30 to 45 minutes, or until some of the liquid has reduced and shrimp turn opaque. Meanwhile, cook rice according to package directions. To serve, spoon shrimp mixture over cooked rice. Makes 4 servings.

Quickly thaw frozen shrimp by placing the shrimp
in a colander and running cold water over them...
ready to cook in no time!

Classic North End Lasagna

Lynda Robson
Boston, MA

We always had lasagna on the table at Thanksgiving...it was a must! This is the back-of-the-box recipe that my mother always used. I wouldn't change a thing!

16-oz. pkg. lasagna noodles, uncooked
1 lb. ground mild Italian pork sausage
1/2 lb. lean ground beef
1 clove garlic, chopped
1/2 c. red wine or beef broth
1 T. dried oregano
1/2 t. salt

24-oz. jar pasta sauce, divided
15-oz. container ricotta cheese
1 c. grated Parmesan cheese
2 eggs, beaten
2 T. fresh parsley, snipped
1/4 t. pepper
16-oz. pkg. shredded mozzarella cheese, divided

Cook noodles according to package directions; drain. Meanwhile, in a large skillet over medium heat, brown sausage and beef. Drain; add garlic, wine or broth, oregano and salt. Cook and stir for 5 minutes. Stir in pasta sauce; simmer over low heat for 15 minutes, stirring occasionally. In a bowl, combine ricotta cheese, Parmesan cheese, eggs, parsley and pepper; mix well. Spread 3/4 cup sauce mixture in a greased deep 13"x9" baking pan. Layer with half of the noodles, half of ricotta cheese mixture, half of sauce mixture and half of mozzarella cheese. Repeat layering. Bake, uncovered, at 350 degrees for 30 minutes, or until hot and bubbly. Let stand 10 minutes before slicing. Serves 8.

Make the children's table fun with special touches. Cover the table with brown paper. Add crayons for coloring and sugar cone "cornucopias" filled with snack mix to munch on. Kids will beg to sit there!

Creamy Spinach Sausage Pasta

Sherry Hallfors
Las Vegas, NV

Introducing spinach to one of my children was no easy task...
but now she asks for this as her birthday dish every year!

16-oz. pkg. ziti pasta, uncooked
1 lb. ground sweet Italian pork
   sausage
1 c. onion, finely chopped
10-oz. pkg. frozen creamed
   spinach, thawed

14-1/2 oz. can diced tomatoes
8-oz. pkg. cream cheese,
   softened
8-oz. pkg. shredded mozzarella
   cheese, divided

Cook pasta according to package directions; drain and transfer to a lightly greased 13"x9" baking pan. Meanwhile, in a large saucepan, cook sausage and onion over medium heat until sausage is no longer pink. Stir in spinach, tomatoes with juice, cream cheese and half of mozzarella cheese. Cook and stir until cheeses are melted; add sausage mixture to pasta and mix gently. Cover and bake at 350 degrees for 35 minutes. Uncover and sprinkle with remaining cheese. Bake, uncovered, for 10 minutes, or until cheese is melted. Serves 4.

Start a family tradition...have a candlelight dinner once a week with your children. A table set with lit tapers, snowy-white napkins and the best china will let your kids know they are special.

Turkey, Black Bean & Sweet Potato Tacos

Linda Peterson
Mason, MI

Bored with the same ol' tacos? These are packed with delicious fresh ingredients! Any leftover filling can be frozen for another meal.

1 lb. ground turkey
2 T. taco seasoning mix
1/2 c. tomato sauce
15-oz. can black beans, drained
   and rinsed
3 sweet potatoes, peeled
   and diced

2 T. butter, sliced
1-1/2 c. fresh spinach, chopped
1-1/2 c. shredded Cheddar
   cheese
8 to 10 corn taco shells
Garnish: sour cream, salsa,
   guacamole

Brown turkey in a skillet over medium-high heat; drain. Stir in taco seasoning, tomato sauce and beans; set aside. In a lightly greased 13"x9" baking pan, layer as follows: sweet potatoes, sliced butter, spinach, turkey mixture and cheese. Cover with aluminum foil. Bake at 375 degrees for 45 minutes, or until sweet potatoes are tender. Serve spooned into taco shells, garnished as desired. Makes 8 to 10 servings.

Why not host a post-Thanksgiving potluck with friends later in the weekend? Everyone can bring their favorite leftover concoctions, relax and catch up together.

Bountiful
Autumn Dinners

Turkey Day Leftovers Casserole *Jeff Howell*
Minonk, IL

*I came up with this the day after Thanksgiving when we had
lots of leftovers. Add a dish of cranberry sauce on the side.*

3 c. cooked stuffing, or 6-oz.
  pkg. chicken stuffing mix,
  prepared
2 to 3 c. cooked turkey, chopped
  or shredded
1-1/2 to 2 c. turkey gravy
2 c. green bean casserole or
  cooked green beans

4 c. mashed potatoes
2 eggs, beaten
1/4 c. milk
1 c. biscuit baking mix
Garnish: shredded Swiss cheese

Spread stuffing evenly in a 13"x9" baking pan sprayed with non-stick
vegetable spray. Layer turkey over stuffing; spoon gravy over turkey.
Layer with green beans and mashed potatoes; set aside. In a bowl, stir
together eggs, milk and biscuit mix; spread batter evenly over potatoes.
Sprinkle with cheese. Bake, uncovered, at 400 degrees for 30 to
35 minutes, until hot and cheese is melted. Makes 6 to 8 servings.

Something Different
Shepherd's Pie

Duane Foote
Portage, MI

This recipe is easy to prepare and a dish everyone will enjoy.

1 lb. ground beef
10-3/4 oz. can cream of celery
  soup
1/2 c. milk

4-oz. can sliced mushrooms,
  drained
3 c. mashed potatoes
2 c. French fried onions

Brown beef in a skillet over medium heat; drain well. Blend in soup,
milk and mushrooms. Spread mixture in a greased 8"x8" baking pan.
Spread mashed potatoes on top; top with onions. Bake, uncovered, at
350 degrees for 30 minutes. Makes 4 to 6 servings.

Quick Shrimp Boil

Angela Henderson
Claremore, OK

My husband and I used to eat at a place in Tulsa called "The Cajun Boiling Pot" where this meal was the staple. They'd bring out a huge pot, dump everything on the table and we'd go to town. When it closed, my husband asked me to figure out how to fix it. Turns out it's ready and on the table in under 30 minutes. Definitely a go-to meal in our house! Serve with sliced French bread.

12-oz. bottle regular or
   non-alcoholic beer
2 c. water
2 to 3 T. seafood seasoning,
   to taste
1 T. salt
1 onion, quartered
1 lb. new redskin or Yukon gold
   potatoes

9 ears frozen mini corn on
   the cob, thawed
1 lb. smoked turkey sausage,
   cut into 1-inch chunks
2 lbs. frozen uncooked shrimp
   in shells
1/2 c. butter, melted

In a large Dutch oven over high heat, combine beer, water, salt and seasoning. Bring to a boil; add onion and potatoes. Boil until almost tender, about 10 minutes. Add corn and sausage; heat through. Add shrimp; cook just until pink. To serve, drain in a colander. Turn out onto a large serving platter, or directly onto brown paper spread on the dinner table. Serve with Cocktail Sauce and melted butter in individual bowls. Serves 6.

Cocktail Sauce:

2 c. catsup
3 to 4 T. horseradish sauce,
   to taste

2 T. lemon juice
Optional: hot pepper sauce
   to taste

Mix together catsup, horseradish, lemon juice and a couple shakes of hot pepper sauce, if desired.

*Vintage-style tea towels make whimsical oversized napkins...
handy for messy-but-tasty foods!*

Seafood Dish Delight

Jo Ann Belovitch
Stratford, CT

A delicious and elegant dish that's a snap to make. Use half shrimp and half scallops, if you like...dress it up with curly cavatappi pasta.

16-oz. pkg. rotini pasta,
   uncooked
6 T. butter
1 bunch green onions, chopped
2 T. shrimp seasoning or
   Old Bay seasoning

1/4 t. salt
1/4 t. pepper
1/8 t. garlic powder
1 lb. fresh shrimp or scallops,
   cleaned
1 c. whipping cream

Cook pasta according to package directions; drain and transfer to a serving bowl. Meanwhile, melt butter in a skillet over medium heat. Add green onions and seasonings; cook until tender. Add shrimp or scallops and a little more shrimp seasoning to taste. Cook until seafood is opaque. Reduce heat to low; stir in cream and heat through. Add to cooked pasta and stir. Serve hot. Makes 4 to 6 servings.

Serve a tasty dill butter with crisp bread sticks. Soften 1/2 cup butter, then blend in 2 teaspoons dill weed, 2 teaspoons fresh chives and one teaspoon lemon juice. Great with seafood!

Kaye's Ham Loaf

Patricia Parker
Cabool, MO

I have 30 first cousins on my daddy's side of the family. We have yearly Thanksgiving reunions and the family is so big we have to rent a huge facility the size of a gym. Last year 170 family members attended! My cousin Kaye always brought her ham loaf and her coconut cake...my two favorite things that I knew would be there each year. Delicious! Kaye passed away a couple of weeks after her last Thanksgiving with us. She will always be missed.

3 lbs. cooked ham, ground
1 lb. lean ground pork
1 c. milk
2 eggs, beaten

1-1/2 c. corn flake cereal,
    finely crushed
pepper to taste

Combine all ingredients in a large bowl; mix well. Transfer to a lightly greased 13"x9" baking pan. Form into a loaf shape. Spoon Brown Sugar Sauce over loaf. Bake, uncovered, at 350 degrees for 2 hours. Makes 12 to 16 servings.

Brown Sugar Sauce:

6-oz. can tomato paste
1 c. water
1/4 c. vinegar

1/2 c. brown sugar, packed
1 t. dry mustard

Combine all ingredients; mix well.

Come, ye thankful people, come,
Raise the song of harvest home!

–Henry Alford

Autumn Dinners

Spiced Apple Cider Pork Roast

Lori Ritchey
Denver, PA

A wonderful autumn roast that fills the kitchen with fall aroma! Delicious served with my Brown Butter Noodles.

1 T. all-purpose flour
1/2 t. sugar
1/2 t. garlic powder
1/4 t. salt
1/8 t. pepper
3-lb. boneless pork roast

1 c. apple cider
1/3 c. brown sugar, packed
2 t. vinegar
1 t. mustard
1/8 t. ground cloves

In a small bowl, combine flour, sugar, garlic powder, salt and pepper. Rub flour mixture evenly over the surface of roast. Place roast in a Dutch oven; set aside. Stir together cider, brown sugar, vinegar, mustard and cloves in another small bowl. Pour cider mixture over roast. Cover and cook at 350 degrees for one hour and 15 minutes. Serve with Brown Butter Noodles. Serves 4.

Brown Butter Noodles:

12-oz. pkg. medium egg
   noodles, uncooked

1/2 c. butter, or more to taste

Cook noodles according to package directions; drain and transfer to a serving bowl. Meanwhile, in a small saucepan, heat butter over medium-high heat, watching until it comes to a brown color. Remove from heat; pour over noodles. Mix and toss to coat. Serve immediately.

Nothing says "autumn" like a warming mug of spiced apple cider! Pour 2 quarts of cider into a saucepan and stir in 1/2 cup of red cinnamon candies. Simmer over low heat, stirring constantly, until hot and candies are dissolved, about 8 minutes.

Unstuffed Cabbage

Cindy McKinnon
El Dorado, AR

*Cabbage has very few carbs...basically you can eat all you want.
So I started making this and I try to keep it around always. When I
get hungry, this is my go-to food. It fills me up, and it's so good too!*

1 T. extra-virgin olive oil
1-1/2 to 2 lbs. lean ground beef
1 onion, chopped
1 clove garlic, minced
2 14-1/2 oz. cans low-sodium
   diced tomatoes

1/2 c. water
8-oz. can tomato sauce
1 head cabbage, chopped
1 t. salt
1 t. pepper

In a large skillet, heat olive oil over medium heat; add beef and onion.
Cook and stir until beef is no longer pink and onion is tender. Add
garlic and continue cooking for one minute; drain. Add tomatoes with
juice and remaining ingredients; stir. Cook over medium heat for
15 to 20 minutes. Makes 12 servings.

Beef-Filled Acorn Squash

Sandra Estes
Akron, OH

*My Aunt Eileen gave me this very tasty recipe that's perfect
for autumn. Whenever I make it, I think of her.*

3 acorn squash
1 lb. lean ground beef
1/2 c. sweet onion, chopped

14-oz. jar Old World style
   traditional pasta sauce

With a 2-pronged serving fork, pierce the skin of each acorn squash
4 times. Microwave whole squash for 8 to 10 minutes, separately,
until soft to the touch. Cut squash in half; remove seeds. Meanwhile,
brown beef and onion in a skillet over medium heat; drain. Add sauce
to skillet; stir well. Spoon sauce mixture evenly into squash halves.
Place squash in an ungreased 13"x9" baking pan. Bake, uncovered,
at 350 degrees for 45 minutes. Makes 6 servings.

Autumn Dinners

Pasta Fasoul Casserole

Sandra Graziano
Mineola, NY

My mother always made this hot dish for us as a
comfort food, especially in the fall and winter months.

16-oz. pkg. elbow macaroni,
   uncooked
1 T. olive oil
1 c. onion, diced
2 cloves garlic, minced
1 lb. ground beef

48-oz. can tomato purée
15-1/2 oz. can red kidney
   beans, drained
2 8-oz. pkgs. shredded extra-
   sharp Cheddar cheese

Cook macaroni according to package directions; drain. Meanwhile, add olive oil to a deep saucepan over medium heat. Sauté onion and garlic until translucent. Add beef and cook until browned; drain. Add tomato purée, kidney beans and cooked macaroni; mix well. Transfer into a lightly greased 13"x9" baking pan. Sprinkle cheese over top. Bake, uncovered, at 350 degrees for 35 minutes, or until cheese is lightly golden. Let stand for 10 minutes before serving. Makes 6 to 7 servings.

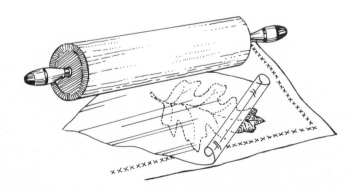

Decorate paper placemats with leaf prints...so easy, kids can do it.
Brush leaves with a little poster paint and carefully lay in place.
Cover with a paper towel and roll lightly with a rolling pin.
Remove the towel, pull off the leaves...so pretty!

Lemon-Garlic Chicken & Potatoes

Jill Daghfal
Sugar Grove, IL

I've been blessed with a wonderful mother-in-law who is also a terrific cook! When I tasted this dish she'd made, it quickly became one of my favorites. I usually like to double the recipe and sometimes use drumsticks or wings instead of breasts. Any way you make it, it tastes terrific!

4 chicken breasts
4 potatoes, peeled and thinly
   sliced
1 onion, thinly sliced
1 T. salt

1/4 t. pepper
3 cloves garlic
juice of 2 to 3 lemons
1/2 c. olive oil

Layer chicken, potatoes and onion in a greased 13"x9" baking pan; set aside. In a small bowl, add salt and pepper to garlic cloves; crush well with a spoon. Stir in lemon juice and olive oil. Spoon garlic mixture over chicken and vegetables. Cover pan with aluminum foil. Bake at 425 degrees for one hour, or until chicken is golden and juices run clear when pierced. Makes 4 servings.

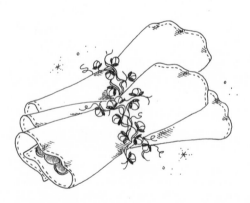

Let the kids help out with the Thanksgiving feast. Something as simple as setting the table and folding napkins means time spent together creating memories.

Honey French Chicken

Nancy Smith
Pompton Plains, NJ

This delicious recipe was given to me at my bridal shower. Each guest brought a copy of her favorite recipe and my bridesmaids put them together in a special cookbook that I still use today, 30 years later.

1-1/2 to 2 lbs. boneless,
   skinless chicken breasts
1/4 c. oil
1/4 c. honey
1/4 c. chili sauce

1/4 c. cider vinegar
2 T. Worcestershire sauce
1 T. garlic, chopped
1.35-oz. pkg. onion soup mix

Arrange chicken in a greased 13"x9" baking pan; set aside. Combine remaining ingredients in a bowl; whisk to blend and spoon evenly over chicken. Bake, uncovered, at 350 degrees for 30 to 45 minutes, turning chicken once, until chicken juices run clear when pierced. May also be made in a slow cooker. Combine all ingredients in a 4-quart slow cooker; stir to combine. Cover and cook on high setting for 3 to 4 hours, or on low setting for 5 to 6 hours. Makes 6 servings.

Turn mini pumpkins into candle holders by cutting out the center and placing a taper inside.

Rice-Stuffed Whole Salmon

Stephanie Coleman
Salt Lake City, UT

I love making this recipe for company. It gets good reviews, even from my children. Sometimes instead of wrapping the fish in foil I'll use an oven roasting bag. If you wish to use brown rice instead of white, add 1/2 cup more water and cook a little longer.

2 T. butter
1/2 c. celery, finely chopped
3/4 c. sliced mushrooms
1-1/2 c. water
2 T. lemon juice
1/2 t. poultry seasoning
1/8 t. dried thyme
lemon pepper seasoning to taste

3/4 c. long-cooking rice,
　uncooked
1/2 c. onion, chopped
2 to 3 T. diced pimentos
3-lb. whole dressed salmon,
　head and tail removed
Garnish: lemon slices, chopped
　fresh parsley

Melt butter in a saucepan over medium heat. Add celery and mushrooms; sauté for about 5 minutes. Add water, lemon juice and seasonings; bring to a boil. Stir in uncooked rice, onion and pimentos. Reduce heat to low. Cover and simmer for 20 minutes. Remove from heat; let stand about 5 minutes. Pat fish dry; spoon stuffing into cavity. Wrap fish in aluminum foil; place in a shallow 13"x9" baking pan. Bake at 400 degrees for 30 to 40 minutes, until fish flakes easily when tested with a fork. Remove upper skin and bones from fish, if desired. Garnish with lemon slices and parsley. Makes 6 to 8 servings.

On Turkey Day, there's really no need for fancy appetizers...just set out a bowl of unshelled walnuts or pecans and a nutcracker! Guests will busy themselves cracking nuts to snack on while you put the finishing touches on dinner.

Harvest
Treats &
Sweets

Bake-Sale Goodie Bars

Vicki Van Donselaar
Cedar, IA

Packed with nuts, coconut and toffee...the name doesn't do these yummy bars justice!

1-1/2 c. chopped pecans
1-1/4 c. shredded coconut
1-1/2 c. toffee candy baking bits
3/4 c. butter, melted
1 c. light brown sugar, packed
1/2 c. sugar
2 eggs, lightly beaten

3 T. milk
1 T. vanilla extract
1-1/2 c. all-purpose flour
2 T. cornstarch
1 t. baking powder
1/2 t. salt

Combine pecans, coconut and toffee bits in a bowl; stir until well mixed and set aside. Add melted butter to a large bowl; let cool to lukewarm. Using a wire whisk, blend sugars into butter until smooth. Whisk in eggs, milk and vanilla; set aside. In another bowl, combine remaining ingredients; mix well and add to butter mixture. Stir until evenly blended. Stir in pecan mixture. Spread dough in a greased 13"x9" baking pan. Bake at 350 degrees for about 25 minutes. Cool completely, about 1-1/2 hours; cut into bars. Makes 12 to 15 bars.

Hosting a bake sale for school, church or scouts? It's great to have a wide variety of goodies. Find out who makes terrific fudge, who won the blue ribbon for apple pie at last year's fair. Ask people to bring their favorites. And it's a great idea to offer some sugar-free desserts!

Special Birthday Brownies

Sarah Taylor
Manchester, IA

Wonderfully delicious! One day I made this recipe and sent a plate of the brownies to work with my husband. I received a personal phone call from one of his co-workers to tell me how much he enjoyed them!

18-oz. pkg. brownie mix
16-oz. container whipped
   vanilla frosting
1 c. dry-roasted peanuts

1 c. creamy peanut butter
2 c. milk chocolate chips
3 c. crispy rice cereal

Prepare brownie mix as directed on box. Bake in a greased 13"x9" baking pan; cool. Spread cooled brownies with frosting; sprinkle with peanuts and set aside. In a saucepan, combine peanut butter and chocolate chips over low heat. Cook until melted, stirring constantly. Remove from heat; add cereal and mix well. Immediately pour peanut butter mixture over brownies. Spread evenly; allow to cool before cutting into bars. Makes one dozen.

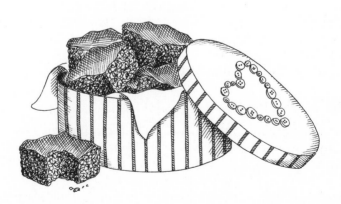

Want to lighten up a favorite brownie recipe? Replace some or all of the oil with canned pumpkin. It makes brownies extra moist and works just as well as oil.

Apple Crisp Cookies

Nina Jones
Springfield, OH

*This yummy recipe won the 2016 "Best Cookie in the County"
prize for me at the Clark County Fair in Springfield, Ohio.*

1 c. butter-flavored shortening
1 c. brown sugar, packed
2 t. vanilla extract
2-1/2 c. old-fashioned oats,
   uncooked
2-1/4 c. all-purpose flour
1/2 t. baking soda

1/2 t. salt
1/2 c. water
1 t. cinnamon
1/4 c. sugar
21-oz. can apple pie filling,
   finely chopped

Combine shortening, brown sugar and vanilla in a large bowl. Beat
with an electric mixer on medium speed until well blended. In a
separate bowl, combine oats, flour, baking soda and salt. Add oat
mixture alternately with water to shortening mixture; stir until well
blended. Combine cinnamon and sugar in a small bowl. Reserve one
cup of dough for topping. Shape remaining dough into one-inch balls.
Roll each ball in cinnamon-sugar; place on parchment paper-lined
baking sheets, 2 inches apart. Flatten each ball with the bottom of a
cup coated with cinnamon-sugar. Bake at 375 degrees for 6 minutes.
Remove from oven; cool on baking sheets for 5 minutes. Top each
cookie with a dollop of pie filling and a sprinkle of Crumb Topping.
Bake another 5 minutes. Cool on baking sheets for 2 minutes; remove
cookies to wire racks. Makes 3 dozen.

Crumb Topping:

1 c. reserved cookie dough
1/4 c. old-fashioned oats,
   uncooked

1/2 t. cinnamon
2 T. brown sugar, packed
1/2 c. finely chopped pecans

Mix reserved dough with remaining ingredients until a crumbly
mixture forms.

Delicious autumn! My very soul is wedded to it.
–George Eliot

Spirited Raisin Cookies

Sue Ellen Morrison
Blue Springs, MO

These cookies smell wonderful while baking...the taste is out of this world! My mother kept these on hand as an after-school treat.

1/2 c. water	1/2 c. powdered sugar
3 T. rum extract	2 c. all-purpose flour
1 c. raisins	1/4 t. baking powder
1 c. butter, softened	1/4 t. salt

In a small saucepan over low heat, combine water, extract and raisins. Bring to a boil; remove from heat. Cover and let stand 30 minutes; drain. In a large bowl, blend butter and powdered sugar; set aside. In a separate bowl, mix flour, baking powder and salt; gradually stir into butter mixture. Fold in raisins. Roll out dough on a floured surface to 1/2-inch thick. Cut with cookie cutters, as desired. Place cookies on ungreased baking sheets. Bake at 375 degrees for 20 minutes. Cool on a wire rack. Makes about one dozen.

A drizzle of white or semi-sweet chocolate makes any homemade cookie extra special! Simply place chocolate chips in a small zipping bag and microwave briefly until melted. Snip off a tiny corner and squeeze to drizzle...afterwards, just toss away the bag.

Popcorn Power Bars

Joann Kurtz
Wichita Falls, TX

These are an easy, healthy snack your kids will love. The ingredients can be changed to suit your taste or needs. Can't have nuts? Use more sunflower kernels instead. Don't care for cranberries? Choose another dried, chopped fruit you like.

8 c. popped corn
1-1/2 c. old-fashioned oats, uncooked
1-1/2 c. orange-flavored or plain dried sweetened cranberries
1/2 c. almonds, coarsely chopped and toasted

1/2 c. unsalted sunflower kernels
2/3 c. honey
2/3 c. brown sugar, packed
2 T. butter, sliced
6-oz. pkg. semi-sweet chocolate chips

In a large heatproof bowl, mix together popcorn, oats, dried fruit, cranberries, almonds and sunflower kernels. Set aside. In a small saucepan, stir together honey, brown sugar and butter. Bring to a boil over medium heat; boil for 2 minutes. Pour honey mixture over popcorn mixture; stir to coat well. Press into a 13"x9" baking pan lined with non-stick aluminum foil. Chill 2 to 3 hours; cut into bars. Melt chocolate as directed on package. Dip the bottoms of bars in melted chocolate; place on parchment paper to set. Store in a covered container. Makes one dozen.

Have a fun after-school snack for the kids. Bake their favorite cookies, fill pint-size Mason jars with cold milk and enjoy some time together while you talk about their day at school.

Treats & Sweets

Caramel Apple Popcorn

Katie Majeske
Denver, PA

Popcorn is our favorite snack and I enjoy trying new
combinations. Nothing says fall like apples and caramels!

10 to 12 c. popped popcorn
2 c. dried apple chips, chopped
1/2 c. butter
1/2 c. light corn syrup
1 c. brown sugar, packed

1 t. vanilla extract
1/2 t. baking soda
Optional: 11-oz. pkg. caramel
    baking bits

Combine popcorn and apple chips in a greased large roasting pan; set aside. In a saucepan over medium heat, combine butter, corn syrup and brown sugar. Cook and stir until mixture boils. Boil without stirring for 5 minutes. Remove from heat. Add vanilla and baking soda; stir until foamy and light in color. Pour butter mixture over popcorn mixture; stir well. Bake at 250 degrees for 45 minutes, stirring every 15 minutes. Spread in a single layer on parchment paper-lined baking sheets to cool. If using caramel bits, melt as directed on package; drizzle over popcorn. Cool, then break apart. Store in an airtight container. Makes 8 to 10 servings.

Stir up some old-fashioned fun this Halloween. Light the house
with spooky candlelight and serve homemade popcorn balls,
pumpkin cookies and hot cider. Bob for apples and play pin the
tail on the black cat...kids of all ages will love it!

Snickerdoodle Bars

Anne Alesauskas
Minocqua, WI

Bars are so much easier to make than cookies, by far! These are super-fast to whip up before the kids get home from school.

1 c. butter, room temperature
2 eggs, room temperature
2 c. brown sugar, packed
1 T. vanilla extract

2-2/3 c. all-purpose flour
2 t. baking powder
2 T. sugar
2 t. cinnamon

Combine butter, eggs, brown sugar and vanilla in a large bowl. Beat with an electric mixer on medium speed until combined. Add flour and baking powder; mix well until a thick batter forms. Spray the bottom of a 13"x9" baking pan with non-stick vegetable spray. Spread batter in pan; use wax paper to pat it down. Combine sugar and cinnamon; sift over the top. Bake at 350 degrees for 25 to 30 minutes, until the top springs back when pressed. Cool; cut into bars. Makes 2 dozen.

My oldest son James has always loved everything pumpkin-flavored. When he was just six years old, he baked his first pumpkin pie from scratch. Everyone in the family loved it and couldn't wait until the next pie was to come out of the oven. Every fall he would bake pumpkin-flavored baked goods for all to try. As he got older, the recipes became more and more intense. By the time he was 12, he had mastered 14 different pumpkin recipes. James was given the nickname "Pumpkin Pookie" by my husband and it has stuck with him since. Pumpkin Pookie is now 24 years old and the family sends him messages every fall wanting to know when their Perfectly Pumpkin Pookie Pie will be ready! Memories of my children are the best memories ever.

–Tressa Frutos, Pomona, CA

Apple Butter Thumbprints

Mary Bettuchy
Saint Robert, MO

These cookies remind me of fall in New England, where I grew up.
I can almost feel the cool autumn breeze whenever I bake them.

1/2 c. butter, softened	1/2 t. baking soda
3/4 c. brown sugar, packed	1/2 t. cream of tartar
1 egg, beaten	1/4 t. salt
1/2 t. vanilla extract	1/2 c. apple butter
2 c. all-purpose flour	1/2 c. sugar

In a large bowl, stir together butter and brown sugar until well
blended. Beat in egg; stir in vanilla and set aside. In a separate bowl,
mix together flour, baking soda, cream of tartar and salt. Stir into
butter mixture until well blended together. Place sugar in a small bowl;
set aside. Scoop dough by rounded tablespoonfuls, shaping into balls.
Roll balls in sugar, coating completely; place on parchment paper-lined
baking sheets. Press your thumb into the center of each ball, creating
an indentation. Spoon apple butter by teaspoonfuls into indentations;
do not overfill. Bake at 350 degrees for 8 to 10 minutes, until just
starting to set up but still soft. Cool on baking sheets for 5 minutes.
Transfer cookies to wire racks and cool completely. Makes 2 dozen.

It's the perfect time of year to share some tasty treats with
teachers, librarians and school bus drivers...let them know
how much you appreciate them!

Peanut Butter Eyeballs

Donna Wilson
Maryville, TN

My kids will not let me give a Halloween party without having these yummy "eyeballs" on the menu. They absolutely love them! Actually, so do I, so I'm happy to make them.

1 c. creamy peanut butter
1/2 c. butter, softened
2 to 2-1/2 c. powdered sugar
12-oz. pkg. white chocolate
  chips

2 T. shortening
1 small tube red frosting or
  decorating gel
Garnish: candy-coated peanut
  butter candies

Combine peanut butter and butter in a large bowl; beat with an electric mixer on medium-low speed. Gradually beat in powdered sugar until thick; shape into one-inch balls. Place on a wax paper-lined baking sheet; refrigerate for one hour, or until firm. Melt chocolate chips with shortening according to package directions; stir until smooth. With a fork, carefully drop balls into chocolate mixture to coat; scoop out and let excess drip off. Return to wax paper; do not let balls touch. Refrigerate until set. Pipe on gel or frosting from center outward to resemble veins; add brown candies for pupils. Keep refrigerated until ready to serve. Makes 2-1/2 dozen.

Carol's Bones

Wendy Paffenroth
Pine Island, NY

This recipe was shared with me at a deacons' luncheon at our church around Halloween. The kids love them...so do the adults!

10-1/2 oz. pkg. mini
  marshmallows
24 to 30 2-inch pretzel sticks

1 lb. white melting chocolate,
  or 12-oz. pkg. white
  chocolate chips

Insert each end of pretzel sticks in a marshmallow. Melt chocolate as directed on package. Working quickly while chocolate is hot, gently dip each "bone" in chocolate several times to coat. Place dipped bones on a wax paper-lined baking sheet to set. Makes 12 to 15 pieces.

Treats & Sweets

Crunchy Caramel Meltaways

Kelly Henkle
Vinton, IA

My dad would make these goodies for me as an after-school treat...I couldn't wait to get home and enjoy one! Now I make them for my own children too.

6 c. corn flake cereal
14-oz. pkg. caramels,
   unwrapped

1/2 c. butter, sliced
1 c. milk
1/4 c. shredded coconut

Pour cereal into a large heatproof bowl; set aside. Combine caramels, butter and milk in a saucepan. Cook over medium-low heat, stirring constantly, until melted. Remove from heat; stir in coconut. Pour caramel mixture over cereal; stir until evenly coated. Drop by large spoonfuls onto wax paper-lined baking sheets; cool until set. Makes 2 dozen.

I was not raised on a farm and had no harvest memories until I was a mother with children of my own. I guess this is why these memories are special to my heart. One of the families from church had a farm and hosted a special harvest-time celebration for our entire church family. This included hayrack rides in the brisk, fall night air and a grilled-out meal of hot dogs & hamburgers with all the fixings. We ate inside the huge barn and sat on top of haystacks. For dessert, there were cookies of every kind. We roasted marshmallows and made s'mores, which was a delight for all who came. This was a moving experience for me and I felt I had been taken back in time. As I looked around at my husband, children and everyone, I saw such joy and contentment on their faces. On this harvest night...for me...time stood still. I have not had such a harvest experience since and will be forever grateful to have had this one!

–Jean Jones, Neligh, NE

Coconut-Oatmeal Cookies

Dianne Selep
Warren, OH

In the late 1960s, when my husband Ed was in the Navy, my mother and I would always send him care packages filled with cookies we had baked. Every time he received a package, everyone would crowd around and help him eat the cookies. These cookies were always the favorite.

2 c. all-purpose flour
1-1/2 c. sugar, divided
1 t. baking powder
1 t. baking soda
1/2 t. salt
1 c. brown sugar, packed
1 c. shortening

2 eggs, beaten
1/2 t. vanilla extract
1-1/2 c. quick-cooking oats,
   uncooked
1 c. chopped walnuts
1 c. shredded coconut

In a large bowl, mix together flour, one cup sugar, baking powder, baking soda and salt. Add brown sugar, shortening, eggs and vanilla; beat well. Stir in oats, walnuts and coconut; set aside. Place remaining sugar in a small bowl. Roll dough into walnut-size balls; dip tops in sugar. Place on ungreased baking sheets. Bake at 375 degrees for 12 to 14 minutes. Makes 5-1/2 dozen.

A large blackboard makes a great bake-sale sign. Pull out lots of colorful chalk to jot down the hours you'll be set up, goodie prices and what your fundraiser is for.

Treats & Sweets

Ginger Drops

Carol Brownridge
Ontario, Canada

The very first time I tried baking cookies, I was a bit nervous. I didn't have any experience baking and wanted to start with something easy, yet still delicious. A friend gave me this recipe knowing that I wouldn't fail as long as I followed these instructions. And she was right! All my family & friends loved these soft chewy ginger cookies. Since then, I've made them for every occasion... birthdays, holidays, or even just on a regular day when I'm craving something sweet, chewy and crunchy all at the same time. I've made them so many times, I've lost count!

4-1/2 c. all-purpose flour	1-1/2 c. butter
2 t. baking soda	2 c. sugar
4 t. ground ginger	2 eggs, beaten
1-1/2 t. cinnamon	1/2 c. molasses
1 t. ground cloves	3/4 c. coarse sugar
1/4 t. salt	

In a bowl, stir together flour, baking soda, spices and salt; set aside. In a separate bowl, beat butter with an electric mixer on low speed to soften. Slowly add sugar, beating until combined; beat in eggs and molasses. Beat in as much of flour mixture with mixer as possible. Stir in any remaining flour mixture with a wooden spoon. Using an ice cream scoop, shape dough into 1-1/2 inch balls. Roll balls in coarse sugar. Place balls on ungreased baking sheets, 2 inches apart. Bake at 350 degrees for 12 to 14 minutes; for chewy cookies, do not overbake. Transfer cookies to a wire rack to cool. Makes 2 dozen.

It's a good idea to begin stocking your pantry in the fall with those things you'll be needing for baking around the holidays... chocolate chips, vanilla, dried and candied fruits, sugar and flour.

Frosted Pumpkin-Walnut Cookies

Leona Krivda
Belle Vernon, PA

*My family really likes these cookies! They're also a must
on my Christmas cookie list.*

1/2 c. margarine	2-1/2 c. all-purpose flour
1-1/2 c. brown sugar, packed	1 T. baking powder
2 eggs	1/2 t. salt
1 c. pumpkin	2 t. pumpkin pie spice
1/2 t. lemon extract	1 c. chopped walnuts
1/2 t. vanilla extract	

In a large bowl, beat margarine with an electric mixer on low speed.
Slowly add brown sugar; beat well on medium speed. Add eggs, one at
a time, beating after each. Add pumpkin and extracts; beat until well
mixed and set aside. In a separate bowl, mix flour, baking powder,
salt and spice; slowly beat into margarine mixture until well blended.
Stir in nuts. Drop by teaspoonfuls onto greased baking sheets, 2 inches
apart. Bake at 375 degrees for 12 minutes. Cool on a wire rack; frost
with Maple Frosting. Makes 7-1/2 dozen.

Maple Frosting:

1/4 c. margarine	2 T. milk
2-1/4 c. powdered sugar, divided	3/4 t. maple flavoring

Beat margarine with an electric mixer on low speed. Slowly add
one cup powdered sugar; mix well. Add milk, flavoring and remaining
powdered sugar. Beat well until smooth and creamy.

Baking a large batch of cookies?
Bake only one or 2 baking
sheets at once, and stagger
them so the hot air can circulate
around them. Rotate baking sheets
halfway through baking time...your
cookies will be perfectly baked!

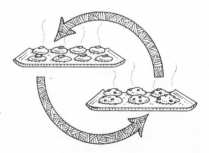

Harvest Spice Bread
with Maple Butter

Debra Hundley
Barron, WI

*I love to bake this bread on a crisp autumn day. It makes your
kitchen smell wonderful with all the scents of the season.*

1/4 c. butter, softened	2 t. baking powder
3/4 c. sugar	1 t. cinnamon
2 eggs	1/2 t. nutmeg
1/2 t. vanilla extract	1/2 t. allspice
1/2 c. sour cream	1/4 t. salt
1 c. all-purpose flour	1/3 c. milk
1/2 c. whole-wheat flour	Optional: 1/2 c. chopped nuts

Preheat oven 350

In a large bowl, beat butter and sugar until light and fluffy. Add
eggs, one at a time, beating well after each. Beat in vanilla and sour
cream; set aside. In a separate bowl, combine flours, baking powder,
spices and salt. Add to butter mixture alternately with milk; beat just
until moistened. Fold in nuts, if desired. Transfer batter to a greased
9"x5" loaf pan. Bake at 350 degrees for 40 to 45 minutes, until a
toothpick inserted near the center comes out clean. Cool 10 minutes
before removing from pan; cool loaf on a wire rack. Serve with Maple
Butter. Makes one loaf.

Maple Butter:

1/2 c. butter, softened	1/2 t. cinnamon
2 T. maple syrup	

Beat ingredients until blended; keep refrigerated. Makes 1/2 cup.

Tuck a crock of Maple Butter into a basket alongside
a loaf of fresh-baked Harvest Spice Bread...what a
scrumptious way to tell a friend, "I'm thinking of you."

Apple Turnovers

Cindy Jamieson
Ontario, Canada

My mom would often make these turnovers during the cooler fall days. I've made a few changes, to add wonderful warmth to them. They are spectacular served with a scoop of ice cream, a drizzle of caramel sauce and a sprinkle of toasted almonds.

4 Nova Spy or Granny Smith
    apples, peeled, cored
    and chopped
1/3 c. brown sugar, packed
1/4 c. all-purpose flour
1/4 t. cinnamon
1/8 t. nutmeg
1/8 t. ground cloves
1/4 t. lemon zest

1/2 t. lemon juice
1/2 t. vanilla extract
2 9-inch pie crusts, unbaked
1/4 c. milk, divided
2 T. sugar, divided
Garnish: vanilla ice cream,
    caramel sauce, toasted
    sliced almonds

In a saucepan, combine apples, brown sugar, flour, spices, lemon zest, lemon juice and vanilla. Cook over medium-low heat, stirring occasionally, until mixture comes to a boil. Reduce heat to low; simmer until apples are just tender. Cool slightly. Meanwhile, roll out one pie crust on a floured surface, 1/8-inch thick. Cut out 4 dough circles, each 4 inches in diameter; repeat with remaining crust. Spoon 1/4 cup filling to one side of each dough circle. Wet edges with a bit of milk; fold remaining dough over filling, pressing to seal the seams. Cut several small slits in tops of turnovers. Brush turnovers with milk and lightly sprinkle with sugar. Place on ungreased baking sheets. Bake at 350 degrees for 10 to 20 minutes, until golden. Serve turnovers warm, garnished as desired. Makes 8 servings.

Fill a bowl with whole nutmegs and a nutmeg grater.
Guests will love fresh nutmeg in their coffee!

Maine Mashed Potato Doughnuts

Teanda Smith
Saint Albans, ME

These are delicious and a favorite of my family. Made with mashed potatoes, they don't soak up the grease like most doughnuts. You can even make chocolate doughnuts with this recipe.

1 c. plain mashed potatoes, warmed
2 c. sugar
1 c. milk
3 eggs, beaten
2 T. butter, softened
2 t. vanilla extract
5 to 5-1/4 c. all-purpose flour

5 t. baking powder
1/2 t. salt
1/2 t. ground mace
Optional: 1/4 c. baking cocoa
oil for deep frying
Garnish: powdered sugar, nutmeg or cinnamon

In a large bowl, combine potatoes, sugar, milk, eggs, butter and vanilla; beat until smooth and set aside. In a separate bowl, mix flour, baking powder, salt, mace and cocoa, if using. Slowly stir flour mixture into potato mixture. If dough is too sticky, add a little more flour. Roll out dough 1/2-inch thick on a floured surface; cut with a doughnut cutter. Combine powdered sugar and spice in a new paper bag; shake to mix and set aside. Add several inches oil to a deep skillet over medium-high heat; heat to 350 degrees. Add doughnuts to oil, several at a time; fry until golden on both sides. When done, add doughnuts to sugar mixture in bag; shake to coat. Makes about 3 dozen.

Whip up a tasty apple cider glaze for doughnuts. Mix up 2-1/2 cups powdered sugar and 1-1/2 teaspoons apple pie spice. Stir in 1/4 cup apple cider until a drizzling consistency is reached.

Apple Pie Filling

Lori Vincent
Alpine, UT

This is one of my very favorite fall recipes. I love to pick the apples from the tree and immediately come in and make the apple pie filling. It makes the house smell so good! So great to have on hand in the pantry for any time you want a quick dessert.

3 c. water
2 T. lemon juice
7-1/2 lbs. Granny Smith apples,
    peeled, cored and sliced

8 1-qt. canning jars with lids,
    sterilized

Combine water and lemon juice in a large bowl; mix well. Add apple slices; set aside. Meanwhile, prepare Brown Sugar Syrup. Pack apple slices evenly into hot sterilized jars, filling 1/3 full. Add enough Brown Sugar Syrup to cover apples. Repeat layers twice, leaving about 1/2-inch headspace. Wipe rims; secure with lids and rings. Process in a boiling water bath for 28 minutes. Set jars on a towel to cool for 3 to 4 hours, until sealed. Check for seals. Makes about 8 quarts.

Brown Sugar Syrup:

2-1/2 qts. water
2-1/2 c. sugar
2 c. brown sugar, packed
1 c. cornstarch

2 T. lemon juice
1-1/2 t. salt
1 t. cinnamon
1/2 t. nutmeg

Combine all ingredients in a large saucepan over medium-high heat. Cook to a gradual boil, stirring occasionally, until thickened.

Add a sprinkle of apple pie spice to mugs of warm cider...so nice served with dessert.

Perfect Pumpkin Purée

Laura Witham
Anchorage, AK

I love making my autumn dishes that include pumpkin purée. From pumpkin soup to pumpkin pie and everything in between, pumpkin purée is ever-present in my house during the autumn and winter months. This is something fun to do with your kids or even your sweetie on those blustery days and it makes your house smell so festive! Use a pie pumpkin...they have a naturally high sugar content and will taste the best.

2 to 5-lb. pie pumpkin

Cut off top of pumpkin and discard. Cut pumpkin into quarters; remove all the seeds and fibers. Cover a baking sheet with aluminum foil; spray with non-stick cooking spray. Place pumpkin pieces pulp-side down on baking sheet. Bake at 375 degrees for one to 1-1/2 hours, until pulp is very soft. Once pulp is cooled, remove pulp from skin and either mash well or press through a potato ricer. Put pulp in cheesecloth and squeeze out any excess water. Pack pulp in plastic zipping freezer bags. If desired, premeasure and label for specific recipes. Keep frozen up to one year. Yield will depend on size of pumpkin.

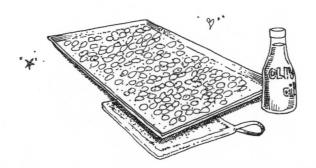

Roasted pumpkin seeds are delicious! Toss the rinsed
seeds with olive oil and spread on an ungreased baking sheet.
Bake at 375 degrees for 10 to 15 minutes, until crisp and
golden. Sprinkle with salt or spice and enjoy.

Whole-Wheat Pumpkin Skillet Cake

Jodi Rhodes
Tolland, CT

This scrumptious recipe came out of the desire for a healthier cake.
For a real show-stopper, top it with freshly whipped cream.

1/4 c. butter, sliced
1/2 c. brown sugar, packed
1 egg, beaten
1/2 t. vanilla extract
1/2 ripe banana, mashed
1/3 c. canned pumpkin
1 c. whole-wheat flour

1/2 t. baking soda
1/4 t. salt
1/2 t. cinnamon
1/4 t. nutmeg
1/2 c. chopped walnuts
1/2 c. semi-sweet chocolate
   chips

Melt butter in a 9" cast-iron skillet over medium heat. Remove from heat; stir in brown sugar. Let cool. Whisk in egg; stir in vanilla. Add mashed banana and pumpkin; stir until blended and set aside. In a bowl, combine flour, baking soda, salt and spices. Add to pumpkin mixture skillet; stir until well mixed. Stir in walnuts and chocolate chips; smooth top with spoon. Bake at 350 degrees for 15 to 20 minutes. Cut into wedges to serve. Makes 8 servings.

Bake up a skillet cookie! Pat your favorite sugar cookie dough into a cast-iron skillet. Bake at 350 degrees for 40 to 45 minutes, until golden on top and slightly browned on the edges. The cookie will continue to bake for a few minutes out of the oven. Turn onto a wire rack to cool slightly and cut into wedges. Yummy!

Treats & Sweets

Cranberry Sauce Cake

Geraldine Weedman
Caldwell, ID

My aunt sent this to me when I was looking for new recipes to try. My mother tried it first and it has become a holiday favorite with our family.

14-oz. can jellied cranberry
   sauce, divided
3 c. all-purpose flour
1 c. sugar
2 t. baking soda
1 t. salt

1 c. mayonnaise-style salad
   dressing
1 c. chopped walnuts
zest of 1 orange
1/2 c. orange juice

Grease a tube pan or a 13"x9" baking pan. Line the bottom with wax paper cut to fit; set aside. Reserve 1/4 cup cranberry sauce for frosting. In a large bowl, mix together flour, baking soda and salt. Add remaining cranberry sauce, salad dressing, walnuts and orange zest; mix well. Stir in orange juice. Pour into pan. Bake at 350 degrees for one to 1-1/4 hours, until cake tests done with a toothpick. Cool; spread with Cranberry Frosting. Serves 10 to 12.

Cranberry Frosting:

1/4 c. reserved cranberry sauce
3 T. margarine

2 c. powdered sugar

Combine all ingredients; mix well.

Sugared cranberries are a sparkling garnish for a holiday cake...
or even for the turkey platter. Simply brush whole berries
with light corn syrup, then roll in coarse sugar.

Grandma Alta Byrd's Devil's Food Cake

Patricia Parker
Cabool, MO

This is the best chocolate cake you will ever taste! The recipe came from my Grandma Byrd, who was born in 1880. She was a wonderful old country woman from the Missouri Ozarks and an amazing cook. This cake recipe has been shared with family & friends for five generations since Grandma Byrd. You will love it.

2 c. sugar	2 t. vanilla extract
1 c. butter	2 t. baking soda
2 eggs, beaten	2 to 3 T. baking cocoa
2-1/2 c. all-purpose flour	1 c. boiling water
1 c. buttermilk	

In a large bowl, combine all ingredients except boiling water; mix well. Add boiling water and beat thoroughly. Pour batter into a greased 13"x9" baking pan. Bake at 350 degrees for 30 to 35 minutes, until a toothpick inserted in the center comes out clean. Cool. Serves 12 to 16.

No buttermilk on hand? Stir one tablespoon vinegar or lemon juice into one cup milk and let stand 5 minutes before adding to a recipe.

Treats & Sweets

Walnut Maple Tarts

Gloria Warren
Ontario, Canada

A variation of a Canadian favorite, butter tarts. Since we Canadians just love butter tarts and maple syrup, putting them together is a natural! If you really want to enter maple heaven, enjoy them with a cup of hot maple tea.

2 9-inch pie crusts, unbaked
1/4 c. butter, softened
2/3 c. brown sugar, packed
2 eggs, beaten

1 t. vanilla extract
1/3 c. pure maple syrup
1 c. walnuts, coarsely chopped

Line 12 tart shells or muffin cups with pie crust cut to fit; set aside. In a bowl, blend butter and sugar until fluffy; beat in eggs and vanilla. Fold in maple syrup and walnuts; spoon mixture into tart shells. Bake at 375 degrees for 15 to 18 minutes, until crust is golden and filling is set. Let cool in pans for a few minutes; remove tarts to a wire rack to cool completely. Makes one dozen.

The leaves had a wonderful frolic,
They danced to the wind's loud song.
They whirled, and they floated and scampered,
They circled and flew along.

–Anonymous

Donna's Kentucky Pecan Pie

Pat Martin
Riverside, CA

The best pecan pie I've ever tasted! Over 40 years ago, my sister-in-law started bringing this pie to our Thanksgiving celebrations. When she moved from California to Florida, she gave me this recipe, written on two blue recipe cards tied together with a peach-colored ribbon. Donna has gone on ahead, but I still make it every year and I sometimes make it into small tarts. Serve with hot coffee or tea...yum!

9-inch regular or deep-dish
  pie crust, unbaked
1 c. light corn syrup
1 c. dark brown sugar, packed
1/3 t. salt
1 t. vanilla extract

1/3 c. butter, melted
3 eggs, lightly beaten
6-oz. pkg. chopped or halved
  pecans
Garnish: whipped cream

Arrange pie crust in a 9" pie plate; set aside. In a large bowl, combine corn syrup, sugar, salt and vanilla; stir well. Slowly add melted butter; stir until well mixed. Add eggs, a little at a time; mix well. Pour into pie crust; carefully place pan on a baking sheet. Sprinkle pecans over top. Place baking sheet on center rack in oven. Bake at 350 degrees for 60 to 65 minutes, until crust is lightly golden and a knife tip inserted in the filling comes out clean. Cool on a wire rack; chill in the refrigerator. Serve with whipped cream on top. Serves 8.

Create a family cookbook! At Thanksgiving, have everyone share their favorite recipes and any memories that go with the recipes. Afterwards, the copy shop can easily make copies and bind them...everyone will want one!

Treats & Sweets

Pumpkin Pie Bars

Patti Bogetti
Magnolia, DE

*This is one of my favorite desserts to make when the leaves
turn colors and the weather starts changing in the fall.*

2/3 c. butter, softened
1 c. sugar
1-3/4 c. all-purpose flour
1-1/2 c. chopped walnuts
14-oz. can sweetened condensed
   milk

15-oz. can pumpkin
1/4 c. light molasses
2 eggs, beaten
2 t. pumpkin pie spice
2 t. vanilla extract

In a large bowl, mix butter and sugar until creamy. Stir in flour and
walnuts until crumbly. Reserve one cup of crumb mixture for topping.
Press remaining crumb mixture into the bottom of a 13"x9" baking pan
lightly sprayed with non-stick vegetable spray. Bake at 350 degrees
for 18 to 20 minutes; remove from oven. With an electric mixer on
medium speed, beat remaining ingredients until smooth. Pour over
baked crust. Sprinkle with reserved crumb mixture. Bake at 350 degrees
for 35 to 45 minutes, until set. Cool in pan on a wire rack; cut into
squares. Store, covered, in the refrigerator. Makes 2 dozen.

I remember in grade school when we spent a week collecting
fall leaves, then took them to school the following Monday.
Everyone shared their favorite leaf and told the class what type
of tree it came from. When everyone had shared their favorite,
we each chose a sheet of colored construction paper and created
an animal using our leaves. It was so interesting to see what
animals my classmates would make from their collection. It is
a memory that I now share with my own children. Every fall
we collect leaves and make leaf animals together.

–Aimee Plesa, Springboro, OH

JoAnn's Chocolate Bread Pudding

JoAnn

A luscious chocolate dessert that's easy to make. Your guests will love it and so will you!

16-oz. loaf French or Italian
    bread, cubed
3 c. milk
1 c. whipping cream, divided
1/2 c. coffee-flavored liqueur
1 c. sugar
1 c. light brown sugar, packed

1/4 c. baking cocoa
6 eggs, lightly beaten
1 T. vanilla extract
2 t. almond extract
1-1/2 t. cinnamon
8-oz. pkg. semi-sweet baking
    chocolate, grated and divided

Spread bread cubes in a lightly greased 13"x9" baking pan; set aside. In a large bowl, whisk together milk, 1/4 cup cream and liqueur; set aside. In a separate bowl, combine sugars and cocoa; mix well. Add sugar mixture to milk mixture; stir well. In a small bowl, whisk together eggs, extracts and cinnamon; add to milk mixture and mix well. Reserve a little grated chocolate for garnish; stir in remaining chocolate. Pour mixture over cubed bread. Let stand, stirring occasionally, for about 20 minutes, until bread absorbs most of the milk mixture. Bake at 325 degrees for one hour, or until set and a knife tip inserted in the center tests clean. Whip remaining cream with an electric mixer on high speed until soft peaks form. Serve pudding warm or chilled, garnished with whipped cream and reserved chocolate. Makes 8 servings.

On a cool evening, invite friends over to enjoy a crackling fire, warm mugs of cider and a favorite movie...always a fall-favorite activity.

Treats & Sweets

Old-Fashioned Indian Pudding

Gail Girard
Cumberland, RI

This is a rich, old-fashioned pudding we used to enjoy when I was a child. It's wonderful to serve on a crisp fall day. It brings back memories of raking leaves and playing with friends.

6 c. 1% milk
1/2 c. butter, sliced
1/2 c. yellow cornmeal
1/4 c. all-purpose or
   whole-wheat flour
1 t. salt
1/2 c. molasses
3 eggs
1/3 c. sugar

1 t. cinnamon
1/2 t. ground ginger
1/2 t. nutmeg
Optional: 1 c. raisins, dried
   cranberries or chopped
   dried apples
Garnish: vanilla ice cream or
   whipped cream

In a large saucepan over medium-high heat, heat milk just to boiling. Watch carefully to avoid scorching. Reduce heat to medium; add butter. In a bowl, mix cornmeal, flour, salt and molasses. Stir 1/2 cup of hot milk into cornmeal mixture. Add cornmeal mixture to hot milk in pan. Cook and stir over medium heat until thickened. In a separate bowl, beat eggs; whisk in 1/2 cup of hot milk mixture. Pour egg mixture into the pan. Add sugar and spices; stir until smooth. Add fruit, if using. Pour mixture into a greased 2-1/2 quart casserole dish. Bake, uncovered, at 250 degrees for 2 hours. Cool for about one hour. Garnish as desired. Makes 8 servings.

For delicious apple pies and cakes, some of the best apple varieties are Granny Smith, Gala and Jonathan as well as old-timers like Rome Beauty, Northern Spy and Winesap. But ask at the orchard...the grower is sure to have tips for you!

Pumpkin Spice Caramel Corn

Lori Vincent
Alpine, UT

I love fall...everything about it! This gooey caramel corn does not disappoint. Our family has been enjoying this for years! Everyone always asks for the recipe. Be sure to use real butter.

10 c. popped popcorn
1 c. butter, sliced
1/2 c. brown sugar, packed
1/2 c. sugar

2 7-oz. jars marshmallow
  creme
1 t. pumpkin pie spice
1 t. vanilla extract

Place popcorn in a large heatproof bowl; set aside. In a saucepan, melt butter and sugars together over medium heat, stirring often. Add marshmallow creme; bring to a boil. Boil slowly, stirring constantly, for 3 minutes. Remove from heat and add spice and vanilla. Pour mixture over popcorn and stir well to coat. Cover bowl while still warm to keep caramel corn gooey. Makes 10 generous servings.

Caramel apple dippers are fun for parties. Slice crisp apples into wedges and insert a treat stick in each. Set out a bowl of caramel dip or topping and a muffin tin filled with jimmies, chopped nuts and other goodies. Everyone can dunk their own apple in caramel, then into a tasty coating. Yum!

Treats & Sweets

Pumpkin Face Cookie Pizza

Sylvia Jacobus
Kent, WA

I've been making this fun dessert ever year since my kids were little. On Halloween they looked forward to this more than anything else. Now, many years later, I'm doing the same thing for the grandkids. They love it too! It's easy to do. And don't worry what to do with leftover candies...I've never had any!

18-oz. pkg. brownie mix
16-oz. container vanilla or
   cream cheese frosting

Optional: orange food coloring
8-oz. pkg. candy-coated
   chocolates

Prepare brownie mix according to package directions given for a 13"x9" baking pan. Spread batter evenly on a greased and floured 12" pizza pan. Bake as directed, watching carefully as less time may be needed. Cool completely. Tint frosting with a few drops of food coloring, if desired. Spread frosting evenly over brownie. Use candies to make your favorite Jack-o'-Lantern face. Cut into wedges or squares to serve. Makes 8 to 10 servings.

Popcorn Autumn Mix

Carrie Kelderman
Pella, IA

This is a fun fall snack to share with friends. It makes a big batch, but will be gone in no time!

8 c. popped popcorn
3 c. corn chips
2 c. crispy corn puff cereal
1 lb. white melting chocolate,
   coarsely chopped

2 c. candy-coated chocolates
2 c. candy corn

Combine popcorn, chips and cereal in a large heatproof bowl; set aside. In a microwave-safe bowl, microwave chocolate at 50% power, 30 seconds at a time, until melted. Stir well and drizzle over popcorn mixture, tossing to coat. Stir in all candies. Spread on a wax paper-lined 15"x10" jelly-roll pan. Chill for 30 minutes; break into pieces. Store in an airtight container. Best if eaten in one to 2 days. Makes 20 servings.

Pineapple-Nut Cake

Renae Scheiderer
Beallsville, OH

*An easy scratch cake you're sure to love. My mom shared
this simple recipe with me, it is a favorite for both of us.*

20-oz. can crushed pineapple
2 eggs, beaten
2 t. vanilla extract
2 c. all-purpose flour

2 c. sugar
2 t. baking soda
Optional: 1 c. chopped walnuts

In a large bowl, stir together pineapple with juice, eggs and vanilla.
Add flour, sugar and baking soda; mix well. Fold in walnuts, if using.
Pour batter into a greased 13"x9" baking pan. Bake at 350 degrees for
40 to 45 minutes, until cake tests done with a toothpick. While cake is
still warm, spread with Cream Cheese Frosting. Serves 12 to 15.

Cream Cheese Frosting:

8-oz. pkg. cream cheese,
    softened
1/2 c. butter, softened

1-1/2 c. powdered sugar
1 t. vanilla extract

Blend together all ingredients until smooth.

Use a linoleum craft knife to carve swirling designs in
pumpkins. Since only the outer surface is carved, there's
no need to hollow out the pumpkins. Even easier...
simply use paint to create the designs!

Treats & Sweets

Choc-Dot Pumpkin Cake

Loraine Sovyn
Saskatchewan, Canada

My family just loves this cake! I have even made it into muffins.

2 c. all-purpose flour
2 c. sugar
2 t. baking powder
1 t. baking soda
1/2 t. salt
1-1/2 t. cinnamon
1/2 t. ground cloves
1/4 t. ground ginger
1/4 t. allspice

4 eggs
2 c. mashed or canned pumpkin
1 c. oil
2 c. bran flake cereal
1-1/4 c. semi-sweet chocolate
 chips
1 c. chopped pecans
1/4 c. poppy seed

In a large bowl, stir together flour, sugar, baking powder, baking soda, salt and spices; set aside. In a separate bowl, beat eggs until foamy. Add pumpkin, oil and cereal; mix well. Add flour mixture to egg mixture; beat until combined. Fold in chocolate chips, pecans and poppy seed. Spread batter evenly in an ungreased Bundt® pan. Bake at 350 degrees for 1-1/2 hours. Cool cake completely before turning out of pan. Serves 10 to 16.

Jazz up a batch of cupcakes for a tailgating party! Spread cupcakes with frosting in one team color, then dot with candy-coated chocolates in the other color. Works great in seasonal colors too.

Apple Cupcakes with Caramel Icing

Tena Huckleby
Morristown, TN

This recipe is my own creation. My family especially likes apples and I like caramel. These cupcakes are perfect for fall!

15-1/4 oz. pkg. golden butter
    cake mix
2 eggs, beaten
1 c. apple cider

1/2 t. cinnamon
1/4 c. light brown sugar, packed
1 c. apples, peeled, cored and
    chopped

In a large bowl, combine dry cake mix and eggs; mix well. Slowly stir in cider. Fold in remaining ingredients; beat well and set aside. Fill 24 paper-lined muffin cups 2/3 full of batter. Bake at 350 degrees for 20 minutes, or until cupcakes test done with a toothpick. Cool cupcakes on a wire rack. Frost with Caramel Icing. Store in an airtight container. Makes 2 dozen.

Caramel Icing:

5 T. butter, softened and divided
3 c. sugar
2 c. milk

1-1/2 c. light corn syrup
1 t. vanilla extract

Grease a large saucepan with one tablespoon butter. Add remaining butter, sugar, milk and corn syrup. Mix well over medium-high heat. Bring to a boil; boil until mixture reaches the soft-ball stage, or 234 to 243 degrees on a candy thermometer. Remove from heat; stir in vanilla. Cool slightly. Beat with an electric mixer on medium speed until creamy.

Conjure up some spooky
Halloween touches...stack cookies
or arrange cupcakes on a black
hobnail cake stand.

Treats & Sweets

Tunnel of Fudge Cupcakes

Sue Klapper
Muskego, WI

I like to see people's surprise and delight when they bite into these chocolaty muffins! Who could resist them?

1/2 c. butter, softened
1/3 c. water
5 sqs. semi-sweet baking
   chocolate, coarsely chopped
5 T. baking cocoa
2 c. all-purpose flour
1 T. baking powder
1/4 t. salt

1 egg, beaten
2/3 c. sugar
1/2 c. milk
1/2 c. sour cream
2 t. vanilla extract
12 milk chocolate drops,
   unwrapped

In a small saucepan, melt butter over low heat. Add water and chocolate squares; stir until chocolate is melted. Remove from heat and cool. In a large bowl, mix together flour, baking powder and salt; set aside. In a separate bowl, combine egg, sugar, milk, sour cream and vanilla; beat with an electric mixer on low speed until smooth. Make a well in the center of flour mixture; pour in egg mixture and cooled chocolate mixture. Beat with an electric mixer on medium speed until well blended. Spoon batter into 12 greased muffin cups, filling 2/3 full. Push one chocolate drop into the center of batter in each muffin cup. Bake at 375 degrees for 20 minutes, or until a toothpick inserted to one side of center tests clean. Cool. Makes one dozen.

Coffee adds a rich taste to chocolate recipes. Just substitute an equal amount of coffee for the water or milk called for in cake, cookie and brownie recipes.

Grandma's Delicious
Pineapple Cheesecake

Mackenzie Remhof
Montgomery, MN

*This is always a favorite for Thanksgiving. All of our cousins
look forward to having this dessert more than the turkey itself!
It is a holiday staple...Grandma never disappoints!*

12-oz. can evaporated milk
30 graham crackers, crushed
1-1/2 c. sugar, divided
1/2 c. butter, melted
3-oz. pkg. lemon gelatin mix

1 c. boiling water
1 t. vanilla extract
8-oz. pkg. cream cheese,
  softened
20-oz. crushed pineapple

Chill unopened evaporated milk overnight; set aside. In a bowl, mix
together cracker crumbs, 1/2 cup sugar and melted butter. Pat into a
13"x9" baking pan, reserving a small amount to sprinkle on top. In a
separate bowl, dissolve gelatin mix in boiling water; chill until slightly
thickened. Pour chilled evaporated milk into another large bowl. Whip
with an electric mixer on medium-high speed until soft peaks form;
set aside. In a separate bowl, blend cream cheese, remaining sugar and
vanilla; add to whipped milk, then add gelatin. Mix all together very
well; fold in pineapple with juice. Pour over cooled crust in pan; top
with reserved crumbs. Chill until set; cut into squares. Makes 18 to
24 servings.

There's nothing like a spicy scent in the air to make a house
feel like home! Pop a few cinnamon sticks and whole cloves
into a small saucepan of water...apple trimmings and orange
peels too, if you have some. Keep it simmering...that
fresh-baked aroma will fill the house.

Apple Pie with No-Roll Pie Crust
*Judy Beal
Dover, OH*

I promise you this is the best apple pie you will ever eat. Our family thinks so. We have been using this recipe since 1979, when my daughter Dee received it in a home economics class her freshman year, and it's still our favorite. The first time she made it, we couldn't believe how delicious it was and how easy it was to make. Now she has a daughter of her own who helps her make this pie.

1-1/2 c. all-purpose flour
1 t. salt
1/2 c. plus 2 t. sugar, divided
1/2 c. oil

2 T. milk
4 to 5 cups Jonathan apples, peeled, cored and sliced
1 t. cinnamon

In a 9" pie plate, combine flour, salt and 2 teaspoons sugar. Add oil and milk; stir until well blended. Use a spoon to shape dough to fit the pan. Flute edges and set aside. Place apples in a large bowl; set aside. Mix remaining sugar and cinnamon in a cup; sprinkle over apples and toss to coat. Spoon apples into crust. Sprinkle Crumb Crust Topping over top. Bake at 450 degrees for 10 minutes. Turn oven down to 350 degrees; bake for 30 more minutes. Makes 6 to 8 servings.

Crumb Crust Topping:

3/4 c. all-purpose flour
1/2 c. sugar

1/3 c. butter, softened
1/8 t. nutmeg

Combine all ingredients; mix with a fork until crumbly.

Who doesn't love a slice of warm, juicy pie? It's always a favorite and so are pie socials! Ask family & friends to bring their favorite pies to share, then be sure to have a pitcher of cool milk and a pot of hot coffee on hand to enjoy alongside.

INDEX

INDEX

INDEX

Find Gooseberry Patch
wherever you are!

www.gooseberrypatch.com

Email

Call us toll-free at 1·800·854·6673

homecoming parades · colorful leaves · BOO!

casual get-togethers · moonlit hayrides

drives in the country · craft fairs

crackling bonfires · community suppers

U.S. to Metric Recipe Equivalents

Volume Measurements

1/4 teaspoon	1 mL
1/2 teaspoon	2 mL
1 teaspoon	5 mL
1 tablespoon = 3 teaspoons	15 mL
2 tablespoons = 1 fluid ounce	30 mL
1/4 cup	60 mL
1/3 cup	75 mL
1/2 cup = 4 fluid ounces	125 mL
1 cup = 8 fluid ounces	250 mL
2 cups = 1 pint =16 fluid ounces	500 mL
4 cups = 1 quart	1 L

Weights

1 ounce	30 g
4 ounces	120 g
8 ounces	225 g
16 ounces = 1 pound	450 g

Oven Temperatures

300° F	150° C
325° F	160° C
350° F	180° C
375° F	190° C
400° F	200° C
450° F	230° C

Baking Pan Sizes

Square

8x8x2 inches	2 L = 20x20x5 cm
9x9x2 inches	2.5 L = 23x23x5 cm

Rectangular

13x9x2 inches	3.5 L = 33x23x5 cm

Loaf

9x5x3 inches	2 L = 23x13x7 cm

Round

8x1-1/2 inches	1.2 L = 20x4 cm
9x1-1/2 inches	1.5 L = 23x4 cm